Joseph Price

Five Letters from a Free Merchant in Bengal, to Warren Hastings

Joseph Price

Five Letters from a Free Merchant in Bengal, to Warren Hastings

ISBN/EAN: 9783337100001

Printed in Europe, USA, Canada, Australia, Japan

Cover: Foto ©ninafisch / pixelio.de

More available books at **www.hansebooks.com**

FIVE LETTERS,

FROM A

FREE MERCHANT IN BENGAL,

TO

WARREN HASTINGS, Esq.

GOVERNOR GENERAL

OF THE

HONORABLE EAST INDIA COMPANY's SETTLEMENTS IN ASIA;

CONVEYING

Some free Thoughts on the probable Causes of the Decline of the *Export Trade* of that Kingdom;

AND A

Rough Sketch, or *Outlines* of a *Plan,* for *restoring* it to its *former Splendor.*

LONDON:

PRINTED IN THE YEAR M,DCC,LXXVII.
REPRINTED M,DCC,LXXXIII.

LETTER I.

FROM A

FREE MERCHANT in BENGAL,

TO

WARREN HASTINGS, *Esq.*

HONOURABLE SIR;

YOUR restoration to power, though by such an accident as that of the death of Colonel Monson, has given great pleasure to the well wishers to the prosperity of Bengal, particularly as it has happened at so critical a time, when the leases of the whole lands of the kingdom are to be renewed. You have now an opportunity (uninterrupted by the cavils of selfish and interested men) to exert your acknowledged abilities in Asiatic financing, as well as to correct any mistakes which you might have made in your former adjustment, by the Committee of Circuit.

WHAT you have done since your accession to the chair, in settling the Company's revenues on a proper basis, and regulating their civil and military expences, is well known to every man at home and abroad, the least conversant in the affairs of this country. I shall draw from it the only argument I think necessary to prove, that it is from your integrity and abilities alone, we can hope to see effected what yet remains undone, to make the natives of this country the happiest people under the sun, and the possession of these provinces the brightest gem in the British crown.

CONVINCED that the extraordinary pains taken by your enemies, to accumulate false and unsupported charges against you, by every unjustifiable means, in the hope thereby to overwhelm you in the opinion of the English nation, will be seen through and despised, I have not a doubt of your triumphing over them from the justice of your cause. Yet should I be mistaken, and the superior ministerial interest, so much boasted of by themselves and agents, should prevail for the present, you must, and will, in the end, be consulted, and advised with, by your Prince and fellow subjects, in order to bring to perfection the great work you have begun.

MY intention in addressing this to you, is with the hope, that some of the hints it contains will

we

be of use, when you shall come to form a plan for restoring the now languishing export trade of this country. Simple, crude, and undigested, as they are, such a penetration as yours will extract something useful from them. I shall, therefore, without further apology, go on to point out, what I think have been the causes of the decline of trade in this kingdom, and the means to retrieve it.

I HAVE frequently heard it affirmed, that the Hindoo, or original native inhabitants of these provinces, were in a better situation with respect to the security of their persons and property, before the English conquered the country, than they have been since. This I constantly denied, from being well convinced, that a genuine native Bengal tiller, or manufacturer, that is capable of judging, if left to his choice, would rather live under the government of the English, than under that of their usurping Nabobs, which the English drove out, or their predecessors the Moguls. A conquest of Bengal! when that phrase is applied to the Hindoo inhabitants, it is improper; to them it has been simply a change of masters. Many millions of them know no difference between the Mahometans who entered their country from the north, and the Christians who came from the south, by the Bay of Bengal. Both have hitherto governed them by the same agents; both left them in quiet possession of their religion, their customs, and their

their manners. A poor simple inoffensive race of tillers and manufacturers, as pusillanimous, trifling, and insignificant, as the women and children of any other country. Conquer these! you never thought of it. But they had placed over them some ages before, by the descendants from that great soldier of fortune Tamerlane, or Timur Begg, a set of task masters, who stripped them of every thing acquired by their industry, except a very bare subsistence. To them succeeded the rapacious revolting Subahs, or Nabobs, whom the English drove out. I have often lamented that Clive did not, after the battle of Plassey, proceed directly to the Caramnassa, whipping before him the motley tribe of freebooters which composed the Nabob's army, until he had driven the whole out of the country. I say I wish he had done this at once, because his neglecting to do it then, has given cause to many evils since, which would thereby have been prevented. Such an entire change of masters, would have been a fortunate circumstance to the real native inhabitants of this country, as it would be easy to make appear: but at present, my time is taken up in attempting to point out remedies for the evils, which the conquest of the country by the English hath brought about.

When the favourites of the Mogul Princes, who had obtained appointments in these provinces, acquired

quired riches, they sent it to Dellhy, or some remote part of the empire, together with the neat proceeds of the revenue, or carried it with them out of the country, if they were recalled. In process of time, these officers of the Emperors, or their descendants, taking advantage of the confusions in the empire, set up for themselves, and became the reigning Princes of the country. The collected treasure was then locked up in their own coffers, and not sent out of the provinces.

DURING the government of the Moguls, and that of the usurping Subahs, the trade of the country remained open and free to the adventurers of all nations, who entered it by the Bay of Bengal, in ships richly laden with silver and gold, which they left behind, in exchange for the wrought manufactures and raw materials, the produce of the country. From whatever section of the globe these merchant-adventurers came, they brought with them some bullion, as their import cargo, whatever it was, would not produce sufficient to pay for the goods they exported. I well remember the nature of the trade to this kingdom, before the English took charge of it; and I believe I keep within the bounds of truth, when I say, that the balance of trade in favour of this country, which was brought to them by the Europeans, and the people possessing the territories on the east and western sides of the Bay of Bengal, amounted to a

million

milliou sterling annually, not one ounce of which was in those days again exported.

Such was the state of the kingdom when the English were obliged, in self defence, to wage war with the usurping Subahs, or Nabobs, whom, in the end, they drove out, and in process of time, took the government into their own hands. In the struggle for power, there can be no doubt, but that the natives suffered in person and property; but whether the Nabob's, or the English army, should prove victorious, a very numerous majority among them would not have given three farthings; ignorant, as they then were, of the good fortune the change brought them. To plough their fields, and weave their cloth in quiet, was all they wished; nor were they capable of judging under the government of which of the contending powers they should be most at their ease.

Suppose a very numerous flock of sheep, which had for some ages been tended by a small number of shepherds, who, for their own interest, covered them tolerably well from beasts of prey, but at the end of each year, stripped them quite bare of their fleece, which they sold, and locked the money up in their own coffers?

Again: suppose that another gang of shepherds, from another country, and of a very different cast,

having

having a quarrel with the old shepherds, attack and drive them out, seize their wealth, and lay claim to the sheep; these last, though greatly inferior in number to their predecessors, yet excel them in every art of managing a flock, in making fences, and defending them from beasts of prey, as well as in the arts of civilization, and acts of tenderness and humanity; will not the last state of such a flock, or, to drop the metaphor, such a people, equally helpless, though not quite so innocent, be better than the first?

I MADE the above digressional remark, purely to shew, that the state of the natives is exactly similar to what it was before the capture, as far as it relates to their customs, usages, civil and religious rights; for of these no attempts have been made to alter them; protection from foreign enemies is infinitely more secure; and their oppressions from government, I am well assured, much less.

I RETURN now to the original cause of the decline of foreign trade, and the reasons why there is great sums of money annually sent out of the kingdom, and very little imported for the purposes of trade, which are the evils brought on by the conquest made of the country by the English, and which I wish to see remedied.

The efforts the Company had made in the late war, to maintain their acquisitions in the East Indies, had, in some measure, distressed their affairs at home: they expected, and they had a right to expect, that their investments from Bengal would be annually increased, from their new funds of wealth, without sending out in their ships, any more bullion from England. After the year 1757, they sent little or none to Bengal: nay, they ordered their servants in Bengal, to send money to Madrass and to China. The war with France prevented the ships of that nation from coming here: and about the same time, the Dutch began to be supplied on easy terms by private people, and of course imported no more money. From this period, to the war with Cossim Ally in 1763, the sums of money sent out of the kingdom, by public and private people, were immense: and the above mentioned Prince is said to have carried with him large sums in his retreat from the provinces.

Notwithstanding the vast exportation of wealth, there was yet left sufficient for a full and unimpeded circulation, for the purposes of commerce. For whether the surplus was secreted by private persons, locked up in the treasury of the Nabobs, carried off by the Mogul officers, or re-exported by the new possessors, it did not affect the welfare of the kingdom, whilst there yet remained sufficient

for

for to answer all the purposes of mercantile circulation.

About the time Lord Clive returned the last time to India, a scarcity of currency was complained of at the presidency, but not much felt in the provinces; and even this evil, so much talked of at Calcutta, the English seat of government, was removed for the present, by throwing into currency a number of gold mahors, of a new standard and value.

It was in the beginning of the government of Mr. Verelst, and during his administration, that the causes of the ruin of the export trade took place, and have increased annually, until some of the best branches are nearly lost.

Lord Clive, on his return to Europe, laid such flattering statements of the situation of the Company's affairs in India before the nation, that it had much such an effect on the minds of the Directors of the Company, Proprietors of Stock, and people in general, as the south sea bubble had some fifty years before. Dividends were increased; stock rose; the ministry put in for a share in the name of government; and the managers in Leadenhall-Street, used every means of stock jobbing chicanery to keep the power in their own hands. Great latitude was given in contracts for goods; and
high

high freight paid for ships, to such as could procure votes, in order to keep the then rulers of the Company in the direction of their affairs. Verelst was called on eagerly, and for God's sake, to send them supplies; and this gave the first idea of buying goods here for the Company with ready money; the most fatal stroke to the trade of this country, that could possibly have entered into the head of man.

Whilst every man in and out of the service, at Bengal, exclaimed bitterly against sending bullion out of the country, they all agreed, that the best mode to relieve the Company, was to increase the cargoes of their returning ships, by opening the warehouse door for the reception of goods, to be paid for with ready money. The Company's standard for goodness in quality, could not be attended to; for that would have shut out almost all that were offered. That line, like the line of rectitude, once forsaken, is hard to be recovered. Goods were admitted of so inferior a quality, that it destroyed the very purpose for which they were bought. The amount of the invoices from Bengal were increased; but the account sale in Europe fell short. Complaints were made; but it was too late; the evil spirit once admitted, introduced others more wicked than himself. The eagerness of the inhabitants to procure goods to sell to the Company, gave cause to the debasing of the manufactures

nufactures all over the kingdom. The Dutch, the French, private adventurers, dealers of all kinds, became the impatient rivals of each other. The ships from Europe could not return without cargoes; and the manufacturers finding a vend for their goods, however ill wrought, took less pains in making of them. How far the evil has since extended, and into what innumerable branches it has spread out, might be thought tedious, if not invidious, to relate. The fact is notorious and plain. I feel no pleasure in dwelling on it, further than is necessary, to point out the causes of the decline of trade, the bad effects of which are now so severely felt.

The Company soon became sensible of the evil tendency of the new mode of procuring goods, and after throwing the whole odium of it on their servants abroad, in the eyes of the nation, gave orders to revert back to the old methods of procuring their investments.

I have said, that though in the days of the Subahs, the people were full as much, if not more, oppressed, than they have been at any time since, yet the sources from whence wealth flowed into the kingdom, remained open. But this could not long be the case after a change of masters. The English never can assimilate with the natives of Bengal; it is not to the interest of their country that

that they should. They come to settle in this country but for a time, and with a view to the bettering of their fortune; when that is effected, they return, and ever will return, if they live to effect the purpose for which they come. A European, and a Hindoo Banyan, the first day they meet, are as much inclined to serve and assist each other, as on the day they separate, though they may have been master and servant for twenty years. The tie arose at first from a view to their mutual interest, in the most gross and pecuniary sense of the word. It is not possible they can have any other. They wrangle about accompts the first month of their acquaintance; they do the same the last week, perhaps day, that they are together. The European hath procured what he came for, and will stay no longer: the Hindoo has made the most of the European's courage, influence, and adventurous mercantile abilities, he possibly could. They part in general, with as little feeling for each other, as a travelling guest doth with his roadside landlord, and take leave of each other in much the same language: '*Adieu, Master Charge-* '*well,*' says the European, '*your entertainment is* '*very good, but your house is confounded hot.*' To which the Hindoo replies, '*God bless your honour;* '*I hope you will recommend me to any of your friends* '*that may chance to come this way.*'

IN such a revolution as that mentioned above, it was impossible but that numbers of individuals among the conquerors, must have acquired large property: They did acquire it; and with it they seem to have obtained the detestation of their countrymen, and the appellation of *Nabobs* as a term of reproach. Yet they took it not from the poor sheep above alluded to, but from their tyrannical task-masters, who had forced the new comers into a war of self defence, which, however, ended in driving away the former shepherds; after which they shared the spoil among themselves.

IT is much easier for their countrymen to abuse them for seizing the spoil, than to prove, that in similar circumstances, they would not have done the same thing: and it is owing to mere accident, that it proved more pernicious in their hands, than in the hands of their predecessors in the government.

THE great wealth which had for a long course of time flowed into Bengal, came from the west; unluckily the late conquerors of the country came also from the west. Possessed of so immense a treasure, they were impatient to transport it to their own country, where alone they could enjoy it. Here again I am induced to form another wish, which, at first view, like that in which I lamented Lord Clive's not having proceeded to the entire con-

quest

quest of the kingdom, immediately after the battle of Plassey, instead of making an unsubstantial peace, wears but a very indifferent appearance; yet the evil consequences which have flowed from its not having been put into execution, will justify it. I wish then that Lord Clive and his Council, had shipped off for Europe, or for China, if you like it better, every *rupee* of the wealth acquired by the *conquest*, or that could have been found in the country, excepting what was barely sufficient for the purposes of commerce and internal circulation; or even to have sunk it in the sea, would have been less pernicious, than the evils which have ensued by the means which have been used to remit it to Europe.

It has been already observed, that soon after the battle of Plassey, the Europeans of all nations ceased to bring bullion with them to Bengal; letters of credit served their purpose full as well. It was the same with the country ships; the owners and captains of which, had only to give tolerable security, that the money they took up at Bengal, should, in three, four, or even five years, be sent to Europe, to obtain what sums they pleased. This facility of obtaining money on very moderate terms, gave rise to a spirit of adventure, as pernicious to the manufactures of this country, as stock jobbing is to fair trade: innumerable schemers arose, who undertook the sending money to Europe, by every rout through which it formerly found its way to India.

India. These unnatural attempts to force back the stream of wealth to its fountain head, had the same effect in mercantile polity, as the attempting to force a great river, with all its supplies and acquisitions of water, after a long course of running, back through the little channel from whence it took its rise: it overwhelmed the schemers with ruin. Had it ended there, it would not have signified much; but its baneful influence extended much further. These new adventurers became rivals to the Company, and to one another. Their eagerness to buy up the manufactures of the country, raised the price, and sunk the real value: for the goods were so much debased, that though they cost more than *thirty per cent.* above what the same goods had formerly cost, yet at the markets to which they were carried, they would not produce any thing like their prime cost, and many of them would not sell at all. At this unlucky period, the kingdom was visited by that most dreadful of all calamities, a famine, which swept away, perhaps, **one fourth** part of the labouring people: this increased the **difficulty of obtaining** wrought goods, and contributed still more to the debasing of their texture, which, by its effects, almost entirely annihilated the former great and beneficial trade of white cloth, from Bengal to the Gulfs of Mocha and Persia.

In the Asiatic section of the globe, the silk and cotton manufactures of Bengal, which were formerly so famous all the world over, had now lost their value, and were no longer sought after: others were found out which answered the purpose full as well, and came much cheaper. Yet the European nations still coveted the goods of this country. First, from a jealousy to one another; secondly, for the sake of the raw materials it produced; thirdly, from their having nothing to substitute in place of the coarse and fine cotton cloths of Bengal, which, inferior as they were, to those formerly manufactured, still sold for a small profit in Europe; and lastly, the English East India Company had no other method of drawing home the tribute from their Indian subjects. The trade carried on in the country vessels, instead of being, as formerly, in favour of Bengal, was absolutely against it. I will select two or three instances from a great number, which I could produce in proof of what I say, and then quit the disagreeable side of the question.

Before the capture of Calcutta, a ship of five hundred tons, belonging to Surat or Bombay, when she made a voyage to Bengal, came full loaded with cotton; the proceeds of her cargo amounted to about eighty thousand rupees; but as this was insufficient to load her home with sugar, salt petre, raw silk, and silk piece goods of various

rious kinds, she either brought with her a letter of credit, the exchange on which was in favour of Bengal, or the balance in cash.

A ship of the same dimensions now, when she has sold her cargo of cotton, lades on board a cargo of coarse rice, and with the balance in money, proceeds to the Coromandel coast, or Island of Ceylon, where having sold the rice, and purchased dollars, she goes on to Batavia for sugar, as that article is not now to be had at Bengal, cheap and in plenty as heretofore. If she proceeds home direct, the returns are made in money, rice, some trifling quantity of raw silk, and silk piece goods, all of which the captain, or supercargo, would willingly make over to any person, that would insure them the difference in the exchange, between Bombay and Bengal current rupees, without other advantage of any kind, to reimburse them for the ship's charges, freight, and premium on money; and this because the markets of Surat and Bombay, are supplied with sugar and raw silk, much better and cheaper from China; a very late and new discovery, which has arose from the neglect to cultivate the first, and in debasing the quality of the last, and highly pernicious to the trade of these provinces: so that if there was not a sale for cotton at Bengal, the trading communication between these two English presidencies, would absolutely be at an end. As to the eastern trade, formerly so advantageous

advantageous to this kingdom, it is carried on almost intirely by the scheming remittance-mongers above mentioned, under every possible disadvantage. Before, and even since, the capture of Calcutta, the trader to the eastward carried with him from Bengal, rice for ballast, a little salt petre, with some piece goods; but Patna opium was the principal article: it was generally good, and cost from two hundred and seventy-five to three hundred and fifty rupees per chest. This difference in the price depended on the demand abroad, not as now, an eagerness for remittance of property to Europe. His cargo sold, the returns to Bengal were made in pepper, some little tin, cloves, dammar, and rattans, but mostly in virgin gold, which contributed much to the enriching of this country.

Our present adventurers hurry out with what they call opium, for which they pay more than double the former price: piece goods are so debased they will not sell, so that now they do not export any; salt petre is become too dear, and rice spoils the opium, that is what they call such, for in fact it is a vile infamous compound, which in a few months dries up to powder. I mean not to indulge in myself the spirit of invective, and here once for all declare, that in my complaining, I have no particular individual in view: but I cannot omit to say, that I feel for the honour of my countrymen, when they sink so much below the

character

character of English merchants, in the miserable arts they permit to be used, to give this adulterated stuff the appearance of opium, in order to impose on the Mallays. Tin, pepper, and other articles fit for the China market, is what they seek, which they put on board large ships, appointed to meet them in certain stations to take their cargoes, by way of remittance to China, where the proceeds are paid to the English, French, Danes, Swedes, &c. for bills on Europe.—The vessel returns to Bengal with a cargo of vile lumber.

HERETOFORE the European ships, exclusive of the Company's goods, brought, under the denomination of private trade, articles for sale, to the amount of, perhaps, ten thousand pounds per ship; the returns were made in different kinds of silk and cotton goods, the manufactures of Bengal. If the captain and officers had money to spare, it was deposited in the Company's cash here, and they were repaid in London. An increase of European inhabitants, and our full proportion of luxury, hath produced vend for double the quantity of those articles of private trade. The manufactures, debased as they are in quality, and raised in price, will no longer answer the purpose of the captain and officers, to carry them to Europe. The Company, I think, admit each ship to pay in about five thousand pounds into their treasury, for bills on Europe. The balance which arises on the sale of the private trade, imported on eight ships, may be estimated to amount annually to one hundred thousand pounds, and this is carried out of the kingdom in cash. It will answer no purpose to multiply particular instances, in proof of the great ruin which is thus advancing with quick and large strides towards us. A good Englishman will feel sufficient mortification in taking one general view of the deplorable difference of the situation in the balance of trade, as it relates to the future welfare of this great mercantile kingdom.

TWENTY-FIVE years ago, vessels, of whatever size or denomination, or from whatever quarter of the globe they imported, brought with them a tribute of gold and silver, which they left behind on the banks of the Ganges.—What a cruel reverse do we experience! There is not a vessel which now trades to this port, from ships of the first magnitude and figure included, down to a paltry salt importing dony from the coast of Orissa, that doth not carry money out of the country.

You, Sir, who are blessed with the generous feelings of a noble heart, who love your country, and know its mercantile interests, will be but too well convinced, that I need not produce other disagreeable instances to prove the truth of my postulatum. Here then let it rest; I turn from it with great pleasure to a more pleasing task; for I
feel

feel as full a conviction on my mind, that the remedy is as certain, and within our reach, as that the ruin is inevitable, if the exportation of cash is permitted to be carried on for a few years longer.

PROMPTED by gratitude for the public good you have done, I would here willingly offer up a tribute of praise in the stile of honest panegyric, but I want language, and the necessary talents to do you justice. Besides, you enjoy a godlike pleasure in going on silently to do your duty, leaving external rewards to the justice of your country.

I SET out with boldly affirming, that the genuine native inhabitants of this country, have had on the whole, their condition bettered by the late change of masters. The lower and most useful sort of them, are an inoffensive, quiet, frugal people, wedded to the soil which they cultivate, neatly and cleanly, in the stile and manner of their forefathers. They have very little knowledge of, or intercourse with, their superior lords. They increase and multiply; plant their field in due season; near unto which, under the shade of some friendly grove of trees, they erect their little huts, which are composed of mud, small sticks, straw, and mats. Simple as they are, by annual repairing, they serve them from generation to generation. From these they watch their growing harvest; and in these they spin their thread, and weave the cloth, to procure

which

which ye come such a distance from home. They render to Cæsar such things as are Cæsar's, and sleep contented with what is left them. Scorpions sting the heart of that man who would disturb their innocent repose, or make their pittance less! Englishmen will not! They durst not do it. Oppressing and destroying the poor naked natives, and the timely sending Nabobs to sleep with their fathers, is mere declamation, critically introduced to serve the ambitious purposes of selfish individuals, by the wretched *Bolts*, and yet more wretched *Dow*. As to population, for which we must depend on the above harmless order of beings, I am certain it is in a much better way than in the days of their former masters; for they are better covered from internal and external injuries. Corn grows as kindly; the silk worm feeds as eagerly, and spins as well: the earth is not more steril, or doth it render up its treasures with greater reluctancy, or in less abundance, to its Christian lords, than in the days of yore, to its Hindoo or Mahometan rulers. The barriers to the kingdom are so well secured, as to insure peace to the provinces to as distant a period as you please. The sea is your own; and there is yet remaining in the country, money sufficient for circulation, and every purpose of commerce. Forgive the injuries you have received, consign the past to oblivion, and boldly begin the work anew. The above, Sir, are the materials you have to work with; nor do I wish them put into

better

better hands. But the work expected from you is great, it is arduous. The prosperity of your mother country, and the happiness of this, in a great degree depend on it. You have the talents necessary; honesty, courage, humanity, and perseverance; use them, Sir; the cause is a glorious one, in which, if you succeed, (and I have not the shadow of a doubt but that you will,) it will raise you to the point to which every noble and generous soul looks up—*honest fame*.

THERE is one, and but one remedy, for all our present, as well as for those evils which we apprehend will come upon us. It is the restoring, as soon as possible, not only the manufactured goods, but also the raw materials for trade, to their primitive goodness and price. You have laid the foundations on which to erect this glorious structure; the moment is favourable to go on with the building. Look down on, and leave behind you, the miserable planners of new taxes, whose parrot jargon means nothing more than raising their interest at home, by forming schemes of drawing money into the treasury, however oppressive to the farmers, manufacturers, and merchants, under the stale and worn out cant, of its being for the interest of our *honourable masters the East India Company*. It is not the Company's only, but the national interest, which is blended in, and interwoven with, the prosperity of Bengal. No narrow, wretched

wretched tide-waiter's plan, will suit the occasion. It must be a scheme in which the whole legal power of the state must be employed, and a steadiness equal to your own to put it in execution.

In the reasoning I may hold, and the hints I may give, I mean to avoid meddling, as much as possible, with the financing branch. I am by no means master of the subject; and if I was, to you my remarks would be useless, as I know you have abilities to form, and steadiness to abide by your own plan, which hitherto hath proved so salutary, and which, with some few alterations, which you have now the opportunity to make, promises so well in future.

There is not in any country in the world, of which I have any knowledge, a more pernicious race of vermin in human shape, than are the numerous cast of people known in Bengal by the appellation of *Sircars*; they are educated, and trained up to deceive; servile, mean, artful, cowardly, and slavish. Their knowledge of writing and figures, and the indolence of their masters, induces a necessity of employing them; but the instant you delegate to them the least degree of power, they are changed into tyrants the most unfeeling and merciless in the universe.

Soon

Soon after your accession to the government, you dislodged a nest of these blood-suckers, and by so doing, gave relief to the general trade of the country, the good effects of which were immediately felt all over the kingdom. This was in abolishing the chowkies placed on the banks of the rivers. They were a grievous and oppressive burthen to the merchants who transported goods from one province to another. These, with the tax on marriages, and some others suppressed since, employed a number of vile Sircar collectors, yet brought little into the public coffers.

There are still remaining other such like grievances, under the denomination of government custom-houses, or inland chowkies. I wish the collections made at these, were compared with the expences for keeping them up, and the balance in favour of the state, set against the hardships, the teizing, perplexities and oppressions, which the people in general suffer from the numerous band of petty collectors, who are always selected from the Sircars above mentioned, I dare believe you would, on a view of such comparative statement, abolish the whole. It must be that the people would find great relief from a general suppression of all kinds of chowky duties. It should be published in every village all the country over; nor should the officers of government be permitted to levy such duty under any pretence whatever. As

things

things are now, the *harpies* above mentioned collect *twelve per cent.* and the state benefits *not one*.

I come next to the duties levied at Calcutta, on goods manufactured in the country, and those expressly for the purpose of exportation, exclusive of the inland oppressions where the cloth is made. The government custom master draws two and one half per cent. the Calcutta custom-house two per cent. the fees of both offices, expence in landing, housing for examination, and reshipping, brings the charge up to five per cent. Can this be right? Our export trade is already extremely decayed, and will not the continuation of so severe an impost sink it still lower? The loading your own articles of exportation with heavy duties, is contrary to the policy observed by all the states in Europe, who pretend to the least knowledge in commercial polity.

Since you, Sir, paid off the Company's bond debt, their revenue is no longer mortgaged. Your land tax and salt duties, after answering every demand of the state for the current year, leave you a large annual balance: you therefore do not want the money arising from these injudicious taxes. But admitting that you do want it, lay it additionally on the imports, all of which, except the article of cotton, had better be burthened than the manufactures of the kingdom, on a great and free exportation of which our whole depends.

We

We are certain great part of our export trade is lost. We can give a tolerable guess from what accidents it has been lost. The evil daily grows upon us. Attempts must be made to check this evil. But as no man can say that his particular plan will answer the intended purpose better than that of his neighbour, it behoves the wisdom of government to attend to every thing which is offered. It costs them nothing: Nor is there any scheme so aerial, but something useful may be extracted from it. The invention of the brazen bull made it clear to the tyrant, that the maker was a horrid monster, unworthy to live. Schemes to lay taxes, and grind the face of the poor, are easy to plan—There are five hundred *Empson's* and *Dudley's* to one *Colbert*. You, Sir, I am confident, wish to fill the national spunge, until its commerce flows again in the natural channel. If I prove so happy as to contribute one single idea towards it, I shall feel my reward; for I love my country, and am interested in the welfare of every branch of the British empire.

I have been assured by a person well versed in the revenue department, that the collections have, since your accession, been put on so certain a footing, that with the least economy in the civil and military departments, there will remain at the end of each year, a balance in the treasury of one hundred and twenty lacks of rupees.

I have

(28)

I have alſo heard that it is a reſolution of government, that one hundred lacks of this treaſure, ſhall be ſet aſide as a ſacred fund, not to be touched but in caſes of extreme neceſſity; and that the ſurplus of each ſucceeding year, after deducting about eighty lacks for the purpoſes of the Company's inveſtment, ſhall be ſhipped off, as hath been the caſe this year, to ſupply the Company's ſettlements at Bombay and China.

Did the export trade of the kingdom flouriſh as it formerly did, and bullion, though in a much ſmaller proportion, flow in from all quarters, as before the conqueſt, a large ſum of money being every year locked up in your ſeparate fund, and ample ſupplies ſent annually to other ſettlements, it would not ſignify much. But as it is but too evident, that the very reverſe of this is the caſe, is it not to be feared, that ſuch locking up with one hand, and ſending abroad with the other, will but too ſoon cramp the general circulation in all the provinces, and render it impoſſible for the farmers to pay their rents? Can it be neceſſary for me to repeat here, that the Company's ſhips carry out every year, more private property in gold and ſilver, than the Company in any period of time imported? Providence, for wiſe purpoſes, which muſt be evident to every reflecting perſon, has denied to this country, mines of the precious metal, which, in various ſhapes, ſerve the inhabitants of the whole globe for ſigns in trade.

A MAN

A MAN of a studious and pious turn of thinking, finds his gratitude raised, and his soul refreshed, in contemplating the goodness of God, in the disposal of what man eagerly seeks after in all quarters of the world, as the good things of this life. He views with wonder and astonishment, the Spaniard and Portugueze, toiling on both sides the great southern continent, in the western world, in quest of silver and gold, which as soon as they have obtained, they fly with it to the northern hemisphere, where, with equal avidity, it is snatched from them, by the English, Dutch, and French, and transported with still more toil, and at greater risk of health and life, to the extremes of the eastern world, and there bartered away for the produce of those distant countries; while the Indian, with still greater avidity and eagerness than the former possessors, commits the glittering spoil, once more, to coffers, chests, or into holes and corners of the earth.

THE legislator will note these providential arrangements as well as the philosopher, and if he is wise, and deserves the appellation of good, he will study, and draw benefit from a knowledge of, but never attempt to counteract them, and will restrain such abuse in individuals, by every legal mode which wisdom can devise.

AFTER the severe drainings to which these provinces have been subject for near twenty years, I much fear we cannot spare so large a sum as one hundred lacks, to be taken out from our poor remaining stock of currency: I also think it unnecessary. The great army you keep on foot, the credit of your arms, and the extreme debilitated and distracted state of all the powers of Hindoostan, from whose situation an invasion of these provinces can be apprehended, secures you for many years against even the fear of an attack on the land side; nor will it (except we fall asleep, and invite them to it) be possible for the French to collect a force at the Islands of France, with which to attack you, without your knowing of it time enough to frustrate such an attempt, either from Europe or in India; and by no other means, or from any other quarter, can you be disturbed. Your fund will, therefore, be a means only to accelerate our dreaded distress, without being of use. Or should you be induced, by your apprehensions in any future time, to think such a stock of cash in hand necessary, I boldly affirm, that by offering the Company's security, in bonds bearing an annual interest of six per cent. redeemable at will, you might collect into your treasury, at a short warning, great part of the private cash in the kingdom.

THE Company's annual income here, has been fixed to a tolerable degree of certainty; and though
the

the civil and military disbursements have been reduced greatly since your accession, yet now you have again the power in your hands, there is still room enough left for further curtailings and savings in both these departments. The money that can be saved, must neither be sent out of the country, nor locked up in coffers, but thrown back into circulation as soon as possible, after it comes to your hands.

I BELIEVE the Company's annual indents for goods of the produce of Bengal, amount to one third more than the quantity that has hitherto been sent home to them. It has been said, that there was neither money to pay for, nor goods to be had, to such an amount. I affirm, on the contrary, that the means are in your hands to furnish both, without the least oppression, and by the most salutary ways imaginable; and that by the year in which the Company's charter will expire, the great purposes undermentioned will be fully answered, may be clearly made to appear.

First.   The Company's debts will be entirely paid off at home and abroad.

Secondly.   The private property now in Bengal, and what shall in future be acquired, shall have an easy and equitable channel of remittance to Europe, by means of bills on the Company.

Thirdly.

Thirdly. That the French, Dutch, and other European nations who trade to Bengal, must, as heretofore, bring with them bullion, **to pay** for the largest part of their cargoes, or find it not possible to trade to this kingdom at all.

Fourthly. That the Company's settlements of Bombay and Bencoolen, may be supplied with **proper and saleable** goods in sufficient quantities, to prevent the necessity of sending out of the current specie, which has been, and continues to be, so very injurious to this country.

I am very sensible that such an apparent alteration in the general plan of conducting the Company's affairs, will require their sanction to give it permanency: but as the experiment may be tried without any additional expence, under the conduct of their present set of servants, I see no objection **they can have to it,** as no possible evil can arise from the trial.

The board of trade must be called upon, to lay before the superior council, estimates of the quantities of goods of each particular sort indented for by the Company, which can be provided at the chiefships, and different aurungs, under their management, in the course of one year, with their

prices

prices set opposite to each article, as well as the full length, breadth, quality, and fineness, agreeable to musters given in by the Company's sorters.

That at the same time they ascertain the sums of money which will be necessary for them to have, specifying in what parts of the kingdom it will be wanting, and the seasons of the year it will be proper for them to have the money, dividing it into two, or, if possible, into three equidistant periods of time, and the number of annoes, or sixteenth parts, of the whole that will be wanting at each of the different aurungs or chiefships.

That the Company's covenanted servants of all ranks, who are employed in the mercantile department, and who shall be deemed by the board of trade to be competent judges of the goods which they offer to provide, shall be permitted, under the regulation hereafter to be mentioned, to engage in contract with the Company.

That the form of the contracts be as simple and plain as possible, drawn up by the Company's solicitor, and have the sanction of the supreme court of judicature.

That there be three principal contractors, whether Europeans, natives, or both, bound jointly, and separately, in every engagement: and in order to prevent their engaging for more than they can provide, it shall be an invariable rule, that a failure in contract, shall preclude the person so failing, from ever being admitted to contract with the Company in future.

THE cloth to be stamped in one corner of each end with a die, on which the names, or initial letters, of the contractors who delivered in the cloth, be engraved, and on one side of it, the name of the sorter who passed it. Lists of the names of the contractors, with remarks on their conduct as Company's merchants, be transmitted, by the first and last ships of every season, to the Company.

THAT imposts and duties on cloth, whether of silk or cotton, of every species and kind whatever, be totally abolished. That all Rajahs, Zemindars, and every kind and species of officers under the government, be prohibited, in the most express terms, from exacting any kind of tax on the weavers and makers of silk or cotton cloth, silk winders, or spinners of thread.

THAT a warehouse be opened in Calcutta, under some such denomination as the Company's ready money sorting godown, and this under the inspection of a committee, composed of three members of the board of trade, the export warehousekeeper, his deputy, and the Company's cloth-sorter for the

time

time being, residing in Calcutta, where the Company's standard musters of every kind of goods in which they deal, be deposited, and a book kept, in which be entered the contract rates that the Company pay for each particular sort. That on a proper application to this committee, any person, whether European or native, be permitted to bring any goods of their own, which shall be compared with the Company's, and if equal in all respects, and the owners request it, the qualifying sorting stamp of the committee shall be put, and he, or they, be permitted to have extracts from the book of rates, in order, if they wish to provide ready money goods at their own risk and expence, they may have every assistance possible to direct them.

That the board of trade be no otherways limited in the quantity of goods to be contracted for, and bought with ready money, than by the Company's annual indent; as it is to be supposed, they will increase their indents, when they find goods are to be had.

This committee should advertise, that they will sit so many days in a week all the year round, to receive such goods as may be tendered, not less in quantity than one hundred pieces of a sort, and every way equal to the Company's musters of the same kind, and pay for them in ready money, or in notes on the treasury.

It will also be necessary to make investments for the markets in India, and for the following reasons.

It has been noticed already, that the eagerness of individuals to transmit to Europe their suddenly acquired and immense wealth, contributed more than any other cause, to the raising the price, and lowering the goodness, of the principal manufactured goods of Bengal.

When the English, Dutch, and French demands of cash for the year were supplied; when the schemers of sending goods to Europe, on Portugueze, Danish, and French bottoms, failed; when, by accounts from constituents in England, it was known that there was a great loss on diamonds, and that gold and silver fell greatly short at home, of its estimated value in India, new methods were to be found out for transmitting money to Europe. Men, unacquainted with commerce, were easily made to believe, that the manufactures of Bengal, sold well at all the ports in India; and provided they could but transport their money, without loss, to Bussorah, Surat, Bombay, Bencoolen, Madrass, China, in short, almost any where out of Bengal, it would not be difficult, from those distant places, to transmit it to Europe, without the heavy discount to which all the other modes were subject. This glimmering of hope set the busy ones to work, and when once the contagion took place,

place, it spread like wild fire. *Rich chiefs of provinces, collectors of the revenue, salt agents, fortunate soldiers, lawyers, doctors, taylors, barbers, and undertakers; all! all! became, or employed, supercargoes and export merchants!*

This rich, spirited, but inexperienced corps, joining themselves to the commercial line, increased the demand for all sorts of goods. Unluckily for the manufactures of this kindom, these sudden and unexpected demands, produced the same effects which they ever have, and ever will produce, a general debasing of the quality of the goods so eagerly sought after. The advantageous terms on which the foreign companies obtained money, induced them to enlarge their homeward bound cargoes. Our Company was straining every nerve, to do the same thing at the same time. All this combining did absolutely, in the space of four or five years, raise the price of the manufactures of Bengal, one with the other, full *thirty per cent.* above the former prices; at the same time it sunk the goods more than *twenty per cent.* in their real intrinsic value. I could descend to such particular instances in support of the above assertions, that would but too well convince the most stubborn Sceptic at a distance, of their being true. We who are on the spot, easily believe what we so severely feel. There is not even the shadow of a doubt remaining, that should our Europe and country ships, contintue to carry

carry out money in the manner they have done, and now do, that a very few years more will drain off so much of our current specie, as to cause a stagnation in the circulation in some parts of the kingdom. No matter where it begins; it will bring on a mortification in that part, that will endanger the whole body.

The relief that you, Sir, formerly gave, by preventing money being sent out of the provinces, to pay the troops stationed in the Nabob of *Oude*'s dominions, has, undoubtedly, postponed our fate for some years. The great savings you made, the first two years after your accession, in the civil, military, and marine departments, have proved refreshing and warm cordials to the drooping spirits of the government; and had you not been interrupted, you might by this time, have done great things towards the revival of the export trade: But, Sir, it languishes cruelly yet; nor will it ever recover, but by bringing back the manufactures to their primitive goodness and price.

Some very spirited and enterprising efforts have been made to recover the trade of the Gulfs, by private persons under your own patronage, but hitherto without effect. The Minerva failed at Suez the former year; the Alexander at Juddah, last year; I wish her better fortune at Suez, this year. Their cargoes were made up of goods manufactured ed in Bengal, and were called in the invoice by their proper names, but the cloth was badly fabricated, and the prices too high. The merchant-adventurers from this port, came home difpirited; and foreigners will have nothing to do with your filk or cotton cloth, for the ports in India.

In this general decay of trade, and defpondency of private adventurers, what is to be our remedy? Why really, Sir, all your efforts, at the expence of your private fortune, will not do. The ftate muft interpofe; and if you undertake to recommend or manage it, fomething yet may be done. Throw not this poor production afide, until you find a better. You ftand pledged to the Englifh nation, for recovering the affairs of Bengal. They look to you for relief: You muft not difappoint them.

The Governor and Council of Bombay muft be written to, to fend round mufters of fuch kinds of filk, and filk piece goods, of the manufacture of Bengal, as will ferve the market of Surat and Bombay, together with an eftimate of their value at thofe ports, and the quantities which they will be able to fell annually of each fort: Thefe muft be provided at leaft to fuch amount, as will anfwer the demand. Bombay will have on Bengal for their annual fupplies. Some fugar and falt petre may alfo be fent. Let them have proper goods

to

to sell, and they will never want circulating currency. But it will be to the utmost degree of folly indiscreet, to continue sending away your own specie to supply their wants.

An investment of proper goods for Bussorah, amounting to four lacks of rupees, for Mocha of three lacks, and one of ten lacks for Suez, should be provided. There is not the least doubt, but if these goods could be had, wrought up to their primitive goodness, and nearly at the prices paid for them about the year 1750, but they would answer every expence of sending, and produce returns in bullion, with an advanced gain, clear of every mercantile charge, of at least *twelve* to *fifteen per cent*. This money, or such part of it as was absolutely necessary for China, might be sent there in cash, or cotton, from Bombay; and I am certain that the markets on that side of India, would take off more well wrought Bengal goods, than would supply money for all their demands of cash at Bombay; leaving the returns from the Gulf, to be brought back to Bengal, or sent to China, as most necessary; which return, I have a confidence, might be increased in a few years, by proper management, to *thirty lacks of rupees annually*.

The settlement of Bencoolen, though very advantageous to the Company in their pepper trade, cannot exist without an annual supply of silver.
Gold

Gold being the produce of the country, they have no currency in that metal; and the inhabitants being in continual want of many even of the neceſſaries of life, they ſend for them to Batavia, which port hath hitherto drained them of all their ſilver. It would be better that the Company ſupply them from home, than permit them to drain more ſpecie from Bengal. But as they often uſe the mode of bartering goods in exchange for their pepper, would it not be as well that they ſend indents and muſters of ſuch goods as they can uſe in barter, and have them ſupplied every year? Theſe goods ſhould be provided in the manner of the other inveſtments, and a charge of *fifteen per cent.* put at the foot of the invoice, in which the opium they want for the uſe of the weſt coaſt, ſhould be included, and an offer made of them to the Company's ſervants at that price. I believe theſe indents would run up to near three lacks of rupees annually. I will give you my reaſons for this opinion hereafter, and conclude theſe rough outlines of the plan by obſerving, that there are many other little drains, which may be ſtopped by means ſimilar to the above.

I AM not one of thoſe deſponding beings who think the kingdom ruined; I know the contrary. I know that the wealth of this happily ſituated country is inexhauſtible; but it lays below the ſurface of the earth. Continue to cover your ſubjects

jects from tyranny and oppression, and they will draw it out, and work it up, ready for your use:

Our evils felt and apprehended, have arisen from accidental causes, to which we did not advert, until we felt the effects: They are now known, and may be removed by a proper application of the means in our hands.

I will suppose that all has been done, or is now in hand to be done, which is necessary or eligible, in the legislative, financing, and political lines. If this be the case, you have no immediate use for your military powers. Let the sword rest in the scabbard, (with a proper attention to discipline, it will not rust,) while you once more look back to your first principles. A view to the advantages of commerce, drew the subjects of Great Britain into this country. Its interest hath been to long neglected: Take it up anew, and you will soon restore every thing to that state, to which the mercantile interest of this kingdom must be brought back, or all your victories, your politics, and your plans of jurisprudence, will avail nothing.

The Company are out of debt here: and some men of good calculating abilities have affirmed, that if the presidency of Bengal continued to send home annually, an investment of eighty lacks of rupees, the Company would be disencumbered of

all

all their difficulties in Europe, before their charter will be out. That an interruption hath been given to your measures, and thereby to an annual increase of such remittance, is to be lamented. It cannot be recalled; but you may again set the wheels a going, and spin the thread anew. Instead of eighty, send the Company home one hundred and twenty lacks of rupees in the goods they indent for, until they have stock in hand, above what is necessary to pay their debts, their current charges, and the dividends on the capital stock. They cannot permit you to draw on them for money: Increase the investment as much as possible, and that impediment will be removed, and with it every evil we now feel or apprehend.

If (as I have heard) your savings amount to one crore, or hundred lacks of rupees, annually, it is twenty lacks more than what is wanting for the current service, including the Company's investment. This surplus will answer the purpose of buying goods for supplying the Company's other settlements, in the manner above proposed, without sending a rupee out of the country.

But yet we want forty lacks of rupees, to increase the Company's investment to one hundred and twenty, in order to enable them to bear being drawn on for four hundred thousand pounds annually, by which means we shall turn the current
of

of private remittance into our own channel, and oblige the other European nations, to bring in silver to pay for their homeward bound cargoes, or cease to come here; as also to put a final stop to the pernicious custom of sending out bad manufactured goods, which hath brought the trade of Bengal, into so ill repute with the people in Asia.

Let subscription books be opened at the treasury, for the receipts of forty lacks of rupees, on the following conditions.

The Company to receive the current rupee at two shillings sterling, and give a receipt for the same, payable in London, at the expiration of one thousand two hundred days from the date, with a simple uncompounding interest of three per cent. per annum.

No person to be permitted, either in his own name, or that of a constituent, to subscribe for more than sixty thousand current rupees for the first year, which shall be paid into the treasury at three distant periods, and in the equal sums of twenty thousand rupees at each payment.

Should the whole not be subscribed the first month after the books are opened, persons who subscribed for sixty thousand at first, shall have permission to add what further sums they choose, until the forty lacks are completed.

I have

I HAVE eftimated the annual receipts, at twenty lacks above what is wanting for the immediate and current ufe of government, and for the Europe inveftment at eighty, as it now ftands, which twenty lacks I propofe to apply to the purchafing of goods for the Gulfs and Bencoolen, for the purpofe of keeping alive the export Indian trade, and the fupplying the Company's foreign fettlements: Not that I think it the whole furplus of each year. Indeed I have been told, that fhould things continue quiet for five years, and the annual furplus be put to no ufe, that moft of the current fpecie of the kingdom, would be accumulated into the Company's coffers. If this is really the cafe, why not at once abolifh the heavy and unnatural weight of taxes on your own articles of export?

No errors in the above reafoning, ought to be employed as arguments in oppofition to forming fome plan for reviving the trade of this port. The writer by no means offers this as a perfect one. If it fuggefts to you, or to the Company, a fingle thought that may be ufeful to this country, and of confequence to Great Britain, he will think himfelf amply rewarded. He is not in the fervice, therefore cannot draw pecuniary benefit from its being adopted, or more than his fhare of the inconvenience, as a fingle fubject, in its being overlooked or neglected. He cannot write for fame; for he owns himfelf deficient in every talent requi-

fite

fite for a writer, whose plan may come to be canvassed in public, but that of speaking truth, drawing his materials from his own observation and experience, and his ideas (such as they are) from his own head. He is even incapable of arranging them in any tolerable degree of order. In short, he knows nothing. But that he feels great mortification at seeing the credit of the manufactured goods of this kingdom decline so fast, and most sincerely wishes to have them restored to their primitive texture and goodness.

From the long internal peace which this country hath enjoyed; from the apparent certainty of its continuing for a course of years, in its present happy state of repose; from the increasing state of the revenue, by which the Company have been made easy in their circumstances; from the facility with which you may raise money to supply such a plan; from the advantage such an increase of the Company's home investment to one third more, will bring to my country, in her present untoward situation with her colonies; from the general satisfaction and content it will give the gentlemen in Europe, who depend for subsistence on their money in India, when they see a door opened for its coming home, on safe and equitable terms; from the certainty I am in, that such a plan, properly supported, will oblige our rivals in the Indian trade, to bring us silver in exchange for our goods,

or,

or, which will do full as well, absent themselves entirely; from the ease with which this scheme may be attempted, without any material risk or considerable expence; from the impossibility of the trade of private adventurers providing a remedy, and the necessity of a public interposition; and above all, from the conveniency of the time to attempt it in; I wish to see some such plan, or a better, if it can be found, tried without delay.

In all I have said, I have carefully avoided giving any offence. I do not mean to give any in what I have yet to say. Cavilling and finding fault, is the province of mock patriots, discarded or would-be statesmen. If I mention what I think an error in management, it is purely to introduce what appears to me a better mode to be adopted in future, and not to reflect on the managers. I wish to see the French, Dutch, Danes, &c. obliged, by good honest mercantile policy, to bring money, or give up their trade in these provinces. On such principles, and in such an open and fair way, I would lessen their trade hither all I could.

The ships the Company send yearly for their eighty lacks of goods, are so filled with trade, public and private, military stores for Madrass and this place, that they cannot by any means, bring with them marine stores sufficient to supply the country ships. The French draw great advantage
from

from this. Now if you increase your investment one third, you want a third more tonnage. And should the Company object to your taking so much money for bills on them, let them send one third of it out in marine stores: The sales will be certain: for our rivals, without having much to do with the country ships, import and sell to the English, full as much as I mention. I would insert a list of the articles which they import, and we want, but the custom-house book can inform you better, or I am mistaken.

If the Court of Directors say, we want no more cloth, nor will we take up any more ships, I beg your permission, Sir, to address a few words to them before I conclude this letter, as I really mean all this in good part, and have no other mode of introduction to them.

HONORABLE SIR and SIRS:

IF you increase your investment from Bengal one third, on the easy terms I propose, you will prevent the French getting money from private persons here, whilst you will saddle them with additional risk and expence, oblige them to bring silver, and at the same time enable yourselves to undersell them at home. You will disable them still

more,

more, by sending us marine stores. But if neither of these proposals meet your approbation, pray attend to what follows.

My meaning is not to offend you. I only wish to circumvent Monsieur in what he is doing to the prejudice of our nation; trading here to our disadvantage. You must, in future, send at least eight ships annually to Bengal. You allow eighty tons of kentledge to each ship, for which you pay freight, on an average, at the rate of twenty-five pounds per ton, and that on six hundred and forty tons, comes to sixteen thousand pounds sterling. Order the captains to land their kentledge, and send them on board the same dead weight in anchors, grapnels, small guns, three and four pounders, with shot, for the country ships, and complete the tonnage with bar iron. You will gain ten thousand pounds by these articles, and Monsieur may keep his to himself. Order home by each ship, in lieu of the kentledge, an addition of one thousand bags of salt petre, and sell it for what it will fetch in Europe. It costs you very little here. It will prevent your rivals from carrying home so much as they do in times of peace, and in time of war. Order the salt petre warehouse at Patna, to be locked up to all but yourselves. If your captains say they cannot shift, or navigate their ships, but with kentledge, tell them it is a mistake, which has its foundation in prejudice arising

from

from long practice. I have been owner of six of those ships, after they had served their time out with you, and the first thing I did, after I bought them, was to sell their kentledge. The ship swam in the Indian Seas very well without it. The same weight of salt petre, will answer the purpose just as well. Should a ship by accident, be kept in India a season or two, to render any particular service, here are old condemned guns enough, which she may have for kentledge, until she be loaded for Europe.

This kingdom, Gentlemen, is very populous, rich in native articles of trade, and wants only a continuance of what it now enjoys, good government. It is all your own; you may mould it as you please. Britain, and Britain only, can defend it; and in return, it will send you annually, a very ample tribute of well wrought goods, sufficient to supply all the nations of Europe; and in so doing, it must be your own fault, if you have rivals in trade to this country much longer.

I am,

Honourable Sir and Sirs,

&c. &c.

Arguments

Arguments to prove the neceffity of an interpofition of the ftate, to fupply a remedy whilft yet in its power, croud fo faft into my mind, that were I to introduce the half of them, they would fwell this addrefs to an enormous fize; nor can I think they will be neceffary. When duty and intereft draw the fame way, other inducements are feldom wanting to put men in action. If ever an individual and a national duty, and an individual and national intereft, were combined together, they are in this inftance. Paft miftakes, at home and abroad, fhould be forgotten; and the whole body of Eaft India Proprietors, Directors, and their fervants abroad, join in one public fpirited refolution, to relieve thefe provinces, by a reftoration of their trade to its former fplendor.

It doth Colonel Dow great honour, that the legiflative powers of his country, in forming the late Act of Parliament for regulating the affairs of the Eaft India Company, feem to have taken many hints from his third volume. But was I in the Colonel's fituation, the pleafure I fhould receive from that, would not by any means counterpoife the pain I fhould feel, on reflecting that I had, by that work, contributed extremely, and very unjuftly, to fix in the minds of my fellow fubjects, a rooted deteftation to their countrymen, who have been ferving the Company in this country. In the digreffive parts of his Hiftory of Hindooftan, there are many infinuations (but not one well authenticated fact) which convey ideas to the mind much to their prejudice. He is now in the command of a very important fortrefs on the frontier of the Bahar province. I have heard that the commanding officer on that station, may make a very handfome fortune in a few years. Nothing could convey to the Colonel's mind, a truer idea of the barbarity of the infinuations which are to be found in plenty in his books, than my hinting in this place, that the means ufed for making the fortune above mentioned, are oppreffive to the people under his command, by obliging them to purchafe their daily provifion at a market, where no perfon can fell any thing, except fuch as are licenfed fo to do by himfelf. But I diflike fuch indirect means of filling a book with infinuations and allufions; it is involving the juft and the unjuft indifcriminately, in one general ruin. There is, I think, a better and more generous way of telling ftories to the public, and that is in plain Englifh, and juft as they happened; in which mode I will relate one or two, and then conclude this Letter.

At the time Dow's Hiftory firft reached India, an Englifh gentleman at the court of the Vizier *Sujah ul Dowlah*, explained to that Prince, the character Colonel Dow had drawn of him in his Hiftory of Hindooftan. The Prince at firft looked ferious, but foon recovering himfelf, laughed very heartily,

heartily, and told the gentleman, that he in some measure deserved the character which Dow had given of him: "*For knowing, as I did,*" said he, "*that he was a Writer of History, I should not have* "*refused him the grant of some Salt Petre Farms in* "*my Country, which he applied to me for.*"

Mahommed Reza Cawn did not keep his temper quite so well in a similar situation; for on his being told what a figure he made in Dow's book, "*This,*" exclaimed the Nabob, "*is ungrateful and* "*intolerable. When that man was first introduced to* "*me, I was informed that he was an ingenious person:* "*I received him as a friend of the gentleman who had* "*recommended him, and, as is our country custom,* "*made him a handsome present, to oblige that gentle-* "*man, who was also a friend of mine. But had I* "*known that he was a drawer of characters, I most* "*certainly would have come up to his price, and have* "*had a good one; it would have cost him no more* "*trouble; and for the matter of fact, he is just as* "*good a judge of one as the other.*"

LETTER II.

LETTER II.

FROM A

FREE MERCHANT in BENGAL,

TO

WARREN HASTINGS, *Esq.*

HONOURABLE SIR;

WHETHER, as your enemies hope and believe, a vessel is now on her way from Europe with dispatches, containing your recall, agreeable to the resolution of a mysterious majority of a Court of Directors, held in May last, or that the Proprietors of East India Stock, have resolution and virtue sufficient, to abide by their reasonable determination, of having you heard in your own defence, before they consent to your condemnation, I know not; nor would a knowledge of the fact, either way, encourage me to go on, or deter me from continuing to address these letters to you;

for

for there is nothing in them, but what pertains equally to every British subject; and your name is placed at their head, as being, from your long experience, intense application, and great abilities, the best, though not the only judge, of the matters they contain.

To secure and increase the commercial connection between Great Britain and her Asiatic possessions, is a matter of such importance to the welfare of the kingdom, that it becomes the duty of every individual Englishman, who can throw new light on so interesting a subject, to do it in the best manner he can. In my former Letter, I pointed out some of the causes of the decline of the export trade of Bengal, and gave you a few hints relative to the means which, I think, would conduce most to the recovery of it. In the present Letter, I shall treat of the trade of India more generally, and attempt to point out how it may be better connected than it is at present, with a view to national utility. That the articles of raw silk, muslins, white and printed cotton cloths, and salt petre, may be procured at Bengal, in as great quantities as the Company shall find vend for in Europe, is an undoubted fact. It is also indisputably true, that the surplus of the territorial revenue, the private property of persons who acquire fortunes in the Company's service, and are willing to pay their money into the public cash on easy terms, for Bills on Europe,

together

together with the sales of the British cloth, copper, iron, and marine stores, which the Company do, and always must send out, will produce a fund sufficient to pay for them, without draining the English nation of one ounce of her bullion.

That the East India trade must be conducted by a company of merchants, with exclusive rights and priviledges, I take for granted; but that this company should have interests subversive of, or running counter to the general interest of the state, is ridiculous to suppose, and folly to assert. The great principle of their constitution is, that as many of their fellow subjects as possible, shall benefit by the institution of such a society; and as few as possible, receive damage or hurt therefrom. It must be for the interest of the state, that every discovery, tending to enlarge, connect, and secure the trade to Asia, should be made public. It cannot, therefore, be for the true interest of the Company, that such discovery should be kept private: yet in writing with the freedom which every man must do, who hopes to do good by what he writes, he lays himself open to the resentment of the Company and their officers. This jealousy of the East India Company, which so strongly prevailed at home and abroad, until the passing of the late Act of Parliament for regulating their affairs, contributed extremely to the keeping the nation in the dark, as to the true state of the national traffic to Asia, and

was

was the principal cause of the established aversion, which the people in general have conceived against their fellow subjects who have acted in Asia. If a servant of the Company, wrote his private sentiments on the state of affairs abroad, or blamed in any shape the management at home, and this was discovered by the indiscretion of his friend, or by his letter being intercepted, which was in the power of the Company, and their servants both abroad and at home, the person so writing was dismissed the service. If a person, not in the Company's employ, was found guilty of this horrid crime, against the reigning despot and his divan in Leadenhall-Street, the protection of the Company was withdrawn, and the culprit pursued by their resentment, until he left the country from pure necessity.

Sir G. Colebrooke was the last of those narrow minded despots, whose miserable management brought ruin on the Company, and disgrace on the nation. How was it possible that the affairs of a great and powerful state, as by their possessions in Asia, the East India Company had insensibly become, should be conducted with success, on a paltry, stock-jobbing, 'Change-Alley plan? The whole of their police was to keep the nation in the dark; to feed their veteran band of annual voters, with favourable jobs and contracts; and to amuse the Proprietary in general, with promises

mises of dividends which they were unable to make good; and in the end, to abuse the nation with frightful tales of the rapacious management of their servants abroad, on whose pretended avaricious peculation, they laid the whole blame of their own misconduct.

The door is now opened, by which the nation may have true information as to the real nature and state of its trade to Asia. Though there is yet a portion of the old selfish, sour, jealous leaven, in and about the heads and hearts of the managers in Leadenhall-Street, which will ferment at the idea of an individual presuming to treat on Asiatic mercantile affairs, which so few of them understand; and was I not so entirely divested of all hopes and fears, as I really am, with respect to their smiles or frowns, I should, perhaps, be deterred, by one or other of those slavish passions, from writing my sentiments with the freedom of an Englishman. This is not a declaration of war, it is only to bespeak peace. I shall avoid to mention the names of individuals, but of such whose general conduct is well known to have deserved national honour, or national contempt, and these I deem legal game, and shall cry them up, or hunt them down, as they occasionally come in my way. If the word conquest, causes the idea of that demi-god *Clive*, covered over with laurels, adding the Asiatic continent to the British empire, to rush into my mind, or the unclassical

word

word *jobbing*, drags there the paltry Knight, arrayed in a bob wig and garb of a broker, pedling away rich provinces, in some dark alley near the Royal Exchange, it will be all one to me; I shall do justice to both, without fear of, or partiality to, any man, or body of men. I address to the name of *Hastings* without his knowledge; but that is to draw the attention of the public, to whom, in fact, I write, and at whose tribunal I wish to be tried.

There are many well meaning men, and good citizens, who think that the government should take the opportunity of the Company's charter being nearly out, to lay the trade to the East Indies entirely open. At no period of time has this notion been a just one, as it relates to national mercantile prosperity. The trade to this distant country, never can be carried on with advantage to the public, but by an incorporated body, with considerable exclusive priviledges, and a very capital stock, to enable them to maintain and support large factories in the different provinces of the Mogul empire. These factories having one common interest in view, contribute to support one another. If, by accident, the ships of the Company fail of a cargo at one, they proceed to another, and are sure to be laden home with goods, within the limited time for which they are chartered. By establishing independent, and consequently rival houses, as is done in Europe, you lose this great advantage.

tage. All the governments in Hindooſtan are entirely deſpotic. There are no written laws, to which the whole body of the ſubjects can indifferently appeal, and by the power of which, each individual, whether native or alien, is defended in perſon and property. The will of the preſent reigning deſpot is the law. And had the European national companies, no other mode of having their property ſecured, than the will of every capricious petty Prince, in whoſe territory they may, for the conveniency of commerce, chance to reſide, nothing could be ſo uncertain and inſecure. The trade from Europe to Aſia, differs in the modes of carrying it on, from that of all other traffic on the face of the earth. The merchant muſt have in him a power to protect his own property, from the rapacity of the Prince in whoſe territory he reſides. The Portugueze, the Dutch, the Engliſh, and the French, ever ſince their firſt reſort to India, by the Cape of Good Hope, have been obliged to carry on their national traffic with arms in their hands. So far arming is proper: but when this neceſſary principle of defence, comes to be changed for offence, the military ſpirit deſtroys the mercantile. To what a low and wretched ſtate are the Portugueze now fallen! How poor, trifling, and contemptible, is their trade to India in our days! It is little better with the French, ſince the Engliſh ſtripped them of their poſſeſſions in the laſt war. Even that little would ſoon be loſt to them, but

for

for that selfish narrow spirit, which yet remains amongst the managers in Leadenhall-Street. The Dutch have firm footing in the Islands of Java, the Spice Islands, and on Ceylon. Whilst they hold those possessions, their trade to India will continue to be of great national importance; when they lose those Islands, their trade to Asia will sink to nothing. They know its consequence, and will, as long as they can, support it with the whole power of their state. It should seem that there is no room for any considerable trade to be kept up from Europe to Asia, but by the maritime powers, as they are called. The Dutch enjoy almost the whole trade on the eastern side of the Straits of Sunda and Malacca, and the English that of all India Proper, to the west of those Straits, except Ceylon. That the French will make some efforts, and that perhaps shortly, to recover a greater portion of the Asiatic trade, I think likely enough. If they succeed, the English may thank themselves. I dare believe, that that truly great minister, Mr. Pitt, (for I hate to remember his title,) hath many times repented the having altered his plan for attacking the Isles of France. He had ordered the British squadron then in India, under the command of Admiral Cornish, to cruise off the Islands of Mauritius and Bourbon, where he proposed that it should be joined by a considerable force from Europe. The Admiral obeyed his orders, and continued to cruise until he had lost a thousand seamen,

and

and quite ruined the squadron under his command. No advice was sent, or, which was the same thing, none arrived to acquaint the Admiral, that *John Bull* had altered his resolution, and was gone to beat his head against Belleisle, on the coast of France, by which means the opportunity was lost, of putting an end for ever to the French trade to Asia. Such opportunities seldom offer in the course of human affairs. The great and penetrating soul of Pitt saw it, and prepared to snatch the lucky moment. What secret spring in the wheel of government it was, which turned him aside from putting an end to the war by such a noble stroke, that would have stabbed to death, the poor remains of the French power to the eastward of the Cape of Good Hope, hath never yet, and perhaps never will transpire.

THE subjects of the European nations above mentioned, ever since they first traded to India, have been at war with the natives, or with one another, as auxiliaries to the natives. Lay open your trade, and you will have a house, established by the merchants in Lombard-Street, at war with another set up by those of the city of Bristol, and both attacked by the honourable society of merchants from Liverpool. Here are no great wholesale merchants, from whom you can obtain a large quantity of ready wrought goods on demand; and for contractors, except you can protect and support

port them, against the rapacity of the officers of their own government, and advance them the money for the goods you want, many months before hand, they never can supply you. Even the East India Company, with all their wealth and all their power, have every year, outstanding balances, remaining due to them from money advanced for goods, which they never can recover, sufficient to ruin private adventurers. Though I speak now of Bengal, the same is true of every other part of India. The Dutch, with all the advantages of a regular established company, interwoven with, and supported by their state; though they gain considerably on the spices, tin, pepper, Batavia arrack, &c. which their ships import annually into Bengal, from Batavia; yet they find it extremely difficult to procure a lading for two, or at most three, ships from Bengal to Europe; and are besides, so great losers on the whole, by their factory at Chinsura, on the banks of the Ganges, that they most certainly would withdraw their servants, was it not that they would, in that case, be obliged to buy their muslins, raw silk, and salt petre, at the port of London. This, and the advantages they draw from the opium which they carry from hence to Batavia, is the only motive to their continuing their Bengal trade.

To me, who am extremely dull of comprehension, it appears very extraordinary, that the Dutch have

have found means to draw a line round the Molucca Islands, which, on pain of confiscation of our ships, and death to the navigators, they forbid us to approach; who will not let us have a clove grain, bit of mace, or single nutmeg, but at their own price; yet are permitted by us, to carry out of this kingdom, as much opium and salt petre as they want. Serve them with the salt petre and opium, in the same manner they do us with respect to the spice trade; put a stop to their obtaining private bills at the amazing advantage of fifteen per cent. discounted by the drawer, and Mynheer will wash his hands of the Ganges, and send to London for the articles of trade, imported into Europe from this country. If this is the situation of the trade to Bengal, of a rich, opulent, and powerful company of merchants, trading to Asia for more than one hundred and fifty years, with every possible advantage, and it really is their situation at present, and has been for some time, how are private English adventurers to benefit themselves, or their country, by the trade to Asia being laid open.

I know some sensible men in Calcutta, who have expressed concern, at the great resort of French private ships this season to the river of Bengal, on a supposition, that it portended certain advantages to arise from that mode of conducting the French Asiatic trade, which would probably increase so,

as

as to become hurtful to the English East India Company. As the importation of fifteen ships from Europe, bearing French colours, in the course of one season, and some of them very capital ones, carried a very formidable mercantile appearance,* I was at some pains to investigate this matter to the bottom; and nothing can be more certain, than that if those private ships depended only on the gains to be made by their outward and homeward bound cargoes, every man concerned in them as owners, must inevitably be ruined. The amount of their invoices out, were in general very trifling; the articles, French cloth, copper, iron, marine stores, and French liquors of all sorts. Most of these articles would not produce the Europe price, and many of them were totally unsaleable. Such puny rivals will private adventurers ever prove to a well established mercantile company: For their homeward bound cargoes, besides the unfavourable proceeds of their outward bound, they brought those pernicious bills on private persons, amounting in the whole to about 150,000*l.* sterling. No provision having been made of goods with which to load them home, they are obliged to take all kinds of cloth, the refuse of the English and Dutch Companies, very ill wrought, and at much higher rates: And the whole amount of the returning cargoes of these fifteen private ships, will

* This Letter was written in 1776.

not equal the returns made to the English East India Company on four of theirs. Are such traders to be envied? Can they continue long to be rivals to the English in this branch of trade? It is impossible. Yet to such a situation (perhaps without knowing, and therefore not intending it) would the advocates for laying open the English trade to Asia, reduce this branch of the national commerce.

I would not trouble you, or myself, with saying more on the subject of these private traders with French colours, could I consider them merely as such; but I conceive the foundation of the voyages of these pretended merchant ships, to be deeper laid than is generally imagined. Those who conceive that the French nation will submit to be mere private traders to Asia, longer than until they are ready, and see a favourable opportunity to have another struggle with you for the superiority, have a different opinion of French faith, and French policy, to what I have.

The internal resources of the French nation, arising from their form of government, and connected situation of the kingdom, enable them to shake off any difficulties under which they may labour, after a long and unsuccessful war, much sooner than any other state in Europe. They have not been idle, or bad economists, for the last fourteen years. The peace of Paris was a bitter pill
for

for them to swallow, nor have they yet digested it. At the Isles of France, Pondicherry, Chanderdernagore, and their other places of abode in Asia, they do what they can to recover their mercantile influence. These settlements are supported by the state, and must continue so to be, until by some favourable stroke, they recover from the shocks received in the last war. Trading in private ships only, will never effect that. I am not of opinion that they will risk a war with great Britain, merely on account of the Asiatic trade; but that they are preparing in all quarters of the globe, to make another effort to recover their mercantile influence, I think is plain enough.

Every one of the private trading ships which come to India, touch at the French Islands. They bring out men, stores, and provisions, to the Islands, and to Pondicherry, for which they receive a freight from the government. Those of them which come to Bengal, carry back, on the King's account, salt petre, rice, wheat, peas, oil, ghee, and other provisions, for which they are also paid a freight. These freights out and home, though but small, yet when added to the little they gain by their trade, will just serve to pay their expences; and keep alive a spirit of mercantile adventure in the nation, until better times. In the interim, the government are forming magazines, and training seamen. When they are ready to strike, they will strike.

strike. But to conceive that the French, or the subjects of any other nation, can carry on a private trade to India, with the least prospect of advantage to themselves, or their country, whilst they are opposed by such opulent and well established Companies as the English and Dutch, shews great ignorance in the nature of the trade, by the Cape of Good Hope to the East Indies.

The Portugueze first discovered the abovementioned rout by sea to Asia. They begged some few spots of ground from the natives, on which to settle themselves at first, bought others, and stole the remainder. The superiority of their discipline, and the use of fire arms, gave them so great an advantage over the pusillanimous, inoffensive natives of Asia, that in a few years, they possessed most of the good trading ports on the sea coast all over India. Had they left at home, their priests and their superstition, and could have prevented the subjects of the other nations of Europe, from following them by the same rout, their empire in Asia, might have become permanent and durable. But their great rivals the Dutch and English, who had laid aside their ridiculous reverence for the see of Rome, came for cloth and spice, and not to make proselytes, or depopulate whole regions, to stock Heaven with unwilling Christians; and being subjects of states better situated, better governed, and of a genius every way better calculated to encourage

courage and support an extensive commerce, they soon circumvented and dislodged the men, who first shewed them the way by sea, to these rich mercantile regions.

BIGOTRY and superstition, which at first infatuated and misled the Portugueze, in their management of their new Asiatic empire, is at length, by a strange turn in human affairs, become of some use to them. In that wild, romantic, and barbarous attempt, of forcing the native Hindoos of all denominations, to become Christians, they formed a numerous body of strange animals, in the shape of human beings, called country born Portugueze Christians. These inhabit the sea coast formerly held by their creators, whose every bad quality they have imbibed, together with their superstition, to which they have added quantum sufficient of their own Pagan rights, which together, make up the most monstrous representation of original Christian purity, that the highest enthusiastic imagination can possibly conceive. These veterans, to a man, adhere to the cause of the Portugueze, and by pedling, picking, and stealing, contribute all in their power, to support those shadows of the antient Portugueze grandeur in Asia; the cities of Goa and Damaun, on the coast of Malabar; Mosambique, on the eastern side of Africa; and Macow, in China. But the surrounding independent inhabitants, the Mahrattas, Coffrees, and Chinese, despise,

despise, and treat them with the utmost degree of contempt. In this low, miserable, and helpless state of their Asiatic settlements, what advantage doth the Portugueze nation draw, from granting licenses to private ships to trade to India? None at all. And in case of a war with either of the maritime powers in Europe, they would be driven out from every one of them in the course of one year.

The Dutch have succeeded to most of the Portugueze original settlements in India. But their trade on the western side is greatly decayed; and but for some mistakes, and I think, unnecessary connivances in the English, would have long since sunk to nothing. I say unnecessary, because they are by no means, an open, generous, spirited rival in trade; heavy, selfish, jealous, and gormandizing. They have engrossed almost the whole trade of the eastern side of India. The English, and the English only, have one presidency, and a few out factories, on the west coast of Sumatra. On these the Dutch at Batavia, have ever looked with a jealous eye. At their desire, and with their connivance, the Count d'Estaing broke his parole, and sailed from the Mauritius, in the late war, with a small force, and destroyed them; and by the same means they will be destroyed, while the French possess the Islands, and the Dutch hold Java, whenever there is a war in Europe between Great Britain

and

and France. I shall say nothing of Balambangam: the plan itself was a foolish one, formed by an enthusiast, and adopted by the Company, more with an intention to serve particular persons, than with a view to public good. But Jones is dead, and Herbert ruined, and the Dutch, like the Devil, grown wiser than of yore. They acted themselves at Amboyna: Agents did the business full as well at Balambangam. If you say this last is conjecture, and may be false, I reply I have a right to risk it. I well know the national character, and mercantile policy, of the people of whom I speak. I saw, and felt, their attempt on Bengal, in the year 1759. The national interest, honour, and the lives of all the King of England's subjects then in Bengal, depended on the activity, steadiness, and undaunted courage, of one great man, and he saved them from *Amboyna part the second*. Alas! poor *Clive!* Accept here a tear of gratitude, shed in honour of thy memory, by a lover of Old England.

Nick Frog could not be made happier, than by seeing his old rival, *John Bull*, become so muddy headed, as to lay the trade of Asia open to all his tenants; because I suppose the wit of man could not devise a scheme, so likely to give the Dutch the ascendency over the English in their trade to India. I could very well describe the treatment English private ships would meet with at Dutch ports,

ports, to which they might resort in quest of cargoes, but it might be thought invidious; for the proverb says it is not proper that the truth should be spoken at all times, and here, I hope, it would be needless: for surely that day will never come, when our rulers shall be so wanting to their duty, as to try such an experiment, as that of laying open the trade to Asia.

The Danes possess a small settlement or two, on the coast of Malabar; Tranquebar, on the coast of Coromandel; and Fort Frederick, in Bengal. Their trade has neither increased nor diminished much for a long course of years. They act prudently and fairly with the natives, have force enough to secure the property of the merchant living under their protection, and their trade being confined to three or four ships in a season, not very richly laden, they manage so as to carry it on very quietly, and within their own bounds. They pay court to the English, and receive many favours from them, who could, if so inclined, annihilate their trade in a month. But *Bull* and *Frog* are animals of different natures and dispositions, and consequently act differently in similar situations. I have no quarrel with the Danes, yet I could wish to see them obliged to bring silver to Bengal, to pay for their goods as heretofore, instead of bills, and this rests with us, and not with them. Simple as is their manner of conducting their trade, weak as in reality their forts and factories are, deprive them of them, and at once their trade is no more. They could not give the merchant, manufacturer, and weaver, the necessary protection, and without it, in vain would they attempt to carry it on by single private ships, or houses of commerce, which cannot exist in Asia, but by force, or at least the appearance of it, and by a body of native merchants and traders, collected together by degrees, lodged and protected within your own districts, and habituated to your customs and manners for a long course of years. Such in general is the situation of the trade, carried on by the several states of Europe, round the Cape of Good Hope to Asia. The Swedes, indeed, have some trifling traffic that way, but it is mostly to China. The Spaniards have hitherto kept possession of the town and harbour of Manilla, with the surrounding islands on the coast of Luconia, from a mixed principle, made up of despotic pride and superstition. Its mercantile advantages are very trifling; for it serves only to convey a few of the manufactures of Asia, to the Spanish dominions in the South Seas. There is a kind of law established among the trading nations in Europe, which prescribes their rout to those islands by the Pacific Ocean; but the law of nature points out a more direct way, by the Cape of Good Hope, and the Straits of Malacca, Sunda, or Batty. Since the capture of Manilla by the English in the late war, the Spaniards have

paid

paid more attention to it. The country round is fruitful and populous. There are vast numbers of that motley race of mortals, whose religion is made up of Christianity and Paganism; but these being a compound of Spaniard and Malay, they are a stouter, and more robust race of people, than those which spring from the Portugueze ingrafted on the Hindoo. The Spaniards will not pay you the ransom money for the town, but would have no objection to return your visit to some of your settlements on the coast of Coromandel. Since the late war, they have prohibited the English from approaching those islands under any pretence whatsoever. For my part, I do not know a place in the world, where a large body of forces may be disciplined, and prepared to act, with greater secrecy, than at those islands. A person the least conversant in the nature of the trade and monsoon winds, which prevail in the Indian Seas, will discover at one view, with what facility a junction could be formed of the French forces at the French Islands, and the Spaniards at Manilla, in order to attack your settlements in India. A Spanish squadron, or single ships, with military stores, and a good corps of officers, may sail from Europe declaredly for the West Indies, and pass the Cape of Good Hope, and so through the Straits of Sunda to the Manillas, where there is no want of stout resolute fellows, religiously attached to the service. Discipline makes soldiers, and here is no want of men,

The

The neighbourhood of that rich, plentiful, and populous town of Batavia, will be no hindrance to such an attempt. As I know the conduct the Dutch held at the Island of Carrack, in the Gulf of Persia, when the English lost their settlement at Bundarick; their behaviour at Batavia, when the French took Bencoolen; and saw the whole of their attempt on Bengal, under Colonel Russell, in 1759; I own I am fully persuaded, that they will never omit an opportunity of shaking our power in India, even though in the attempt, they risked a part of their own. With such numerous, powerful, and irreconcileable mercantile rivals on all sides of you, is this the time proper for trying experiments? Surely no man will answer in the affirmative.

THE ample and permanent territorial possessions now held by the East India Company, give to the English nation, that exclusive right to the trade to Asia, with respect to the other nations in Europe, (the Dutch excepted,) which charters granted formerly to particular societies in each state, were supposed to have conveyed to individuals. What then would be the consequence of laying open the trade to Asia, but the giving back to our rivals, the advantages which, at an immense expence of blood and treasure, we have acquired over them?

The duties, and other imposts, on the Asiatic goods, imported by the Company, bring a neat *million sterling* into the national coffers. It increases annually, and will continue to increase, while proper attention is paid to this beneficial branch of national commerce. Numbers of individuals grow rich by the same means which are used to fill the national spunge: And Montesquieu will tell you, that immense fortunes acquired by merchants in the way of trade, though it increases luxury, is by no means prejudicial in a monarchial state.

The regular forces kept on foot at the Company's different provinces in Asia, amount to sixty thousand effective men; these give the necessary protection to the trade we carry on, and are paid out of the surplus proceeds of the territorial revenue. They are cloathed in British cloth, and are at all times ready to oppose to our European invaders, or Asiatic enemies. A good ministry will watch over the managers of this rich mercantile mine, but be very cautious how they wantonly change the established mode of management.

I really dont know how your systematical writers contrive to keep so cooly close to the matter in hand; here am I now quite at a loss, whether I should return back to my plans for connecting and extending the Company's Asiatic commerce, or now, that I have got hold on the military establishment,

ment, whether I had not better proceed at once to carry on the lines of communication, between the Company's troops stationed at Bengal and Bombay, by extending the chain of posts from Calcutta, by Allahabad, to Agra, to Delhi, to Poonah, and so round by Surat to Bombay; then fly down the coast of Malabar to Anjango; there cross over the peninsula through the kingdom of Travancore, Mysore, all through the Carnatic, to Madrass, and on again to Masulipatan, Ganjam, Cattack, Midnapore, and so home to Calcutta. Here is a pretty little circle for you: Pray, Sir, take the map, and observe how easily all this is to be effected, and how finely it surrounds and secures to you, the whole, or greatest part of the trading inhabitants of India Proper. But I am deterred from mounting a poney to whose paces I have not been accustomed, by observing the ridiculous and contemptible figure a man exhibits, who will be meddling out of his own profession. General John Clavering knows just as much of forming plans for collecting the revenue, providing an investment, dressing opium, or making salt, as I do of marches and counter marches. Prithee, *old veteran*, dismount from that unseemly hobby-horse, which providence hath not given you the talents to manage, and no longer risk the national interest, and your own neck, by obstinately attempting to govern an animal, that stoops to nothing but gentle usage, common honesty, and common sense.

THIS

This last digression, which hath stolen on me I know not how, has sunk my spirits into a kind of state of despondency. I fancy that I see the glorious mercantile edifice, which, for a long course of years, I have been wishing to see perfected, sinking down to ruin, and crumbling into dust.

The perfidious, enthusiastic, and superstitious conduct of the Portugueze, on their first settling in Asia, gave the Princes of the country a very indifferent opinion of the sense and morals of the Europeans, who had found a way by sea to their dominions. The bloody quarrels which soon after ensued, between the first comers and their immediate followers, did not remove their prejudices. They soon discovered, that to gain a point in trade over their rivals, these bold and daring visitors would sacrifice every idea of honour and good faith. The first inducement for bringing about a commercial intercourse between the inhabitants of the east and western section of the globe, viz. a friendly and equitable exchange of the European articles of trade for those of Asia, was forgotten or laid aside. Treaties offensive and defensive, were entered into; and the indolent, pusillanimous Asiatic despot, surrendered the valuable mercantile commodities of his country, to those among the new comers, who could best defend him from, or revenge him of his enemies.

This

THIS joining a spirit for conquest, to the eager mercantile avidity which first gave motion to the adventurers, introduced a new principle of conduct, greatly injurious, if not absolutely destructive, of their true interest. It would lead me too far from the subject which first prompted me to the writing of these Letters, or I could prove by a great number of incontestible facts, that the first cause of the decline of the power of the Portugueze, the French, and of the present debilitated, feeble, declining state of the Dutch commerce in India, was entirely owing to their injudiciously mingling too great a portion of the military leaven in their mercantile polity, and an unnatural ingraftment of military heads on mercantile bodies. I could wish our rulers would seriously consider this matter, and take warning from the fate of their neighbours.

BEFORE the war which terminated at Aix-la-Chapelle in 1748, the English had kept pretty close to their first mercantile principle. So far were they from thinking of making conquests, that they suffered on the coast of Malabar, at Bengal, and in many other parts of India, many injuries and insults, from the native Princes and their officers. The few troops they had, were rather for show than use; and those were stationed within their factories, to cover them from the ravages of freebooters, and not to annoy the surrounding country powers. In this state they carried on an extensive

and

and beneficial branch of trade; protected by the warlike character, and great maritime power, of the state to which they were subjects, until the restless ambition of the French on the coast of Coromandel, called them forth to action. On this stage the great Clive first made his appearance in a military character, and by his example, roused the martial genius of his countrymen, and dragged the cautious, prudent measurer of cloth, from behind the counter to the camp. Their appearance there was become necessary and justifiable; for it was in defence of the priviledges and immunities, which had been granted to them by the Mogul Princes, as a body of English merchants, trading under the sanction of a royal phirmaun to their dominions. The consequences of that war, and the succeeding one with the country powers, are well known; but they have led the English East India Company very far from the original intention, and nature of their constitution, and have opened a wide door for innovation. There is yet time and opportunity, for them to revert back to first principles. Armed thy are, and armed they must remain, in order to keep up the influence they have (I may say) accidently acquired; but there is no necessity for their running the risk of meeting the fate of their predecessors, contemporaries, and rivals in India, by changing their government from a civil mercantile body, into a military despotism. How near they have lately approached to this fatal change, the
conduct

conduct of General Clavering and Colonel Monson at Bengal, and of General Sir Robert Fletcher and Colonel Stewart at Madrafs, are evidence fufficient.

If the placing General Clavering at Bengal, General Carnac at Bombay, and General Fletcher or Colonel Stewart at Madrafs, is to prepare the way for changing thofe mercantile prefidencies into military governments, like Gibraltar or Mahon, or as a preparative for taking the garrifons into the hands of government, and laying open the trade to Afia, I fhall be forry for it; and feel again that difagreeable fenfation, which weighed down my heart, on the firft intelligence we received here, that a civil war had broke out in America. The fons of Britain united, may brave the world to arms. Divided, what will they prove, but the poor fhadows of a declining ftate, whofe name and great actions may, like that of the ancient Romans, be handed down to pofterity, but the government, or the people themfelves, be no more to be found? Or if continuing to exift, will be reprefented as modern Rome, and the miferable Italians, do the old miftrefs of the world, and her hardy veterans. If the Englifh trade to Afia is to be laid open, the Crown muft take poffeffion of the Company's lands, forts, and garrifons. The intereft of the ftate and of individuals, will be different; and though enough may be dragooned out of the natives, to pay the wages of their mafters in fcarlet robes, how is the surplus, should any remain, to be remitted to the English treasury? Not in specie, for we shall have none left: not by private traders, for they will be rivals to one another, and smugglers in the state. Those of them will be the most favoured, who shall find the means to stand highest in the opinion of the military despot, presiding at each of the presidencies. Hath it ever yet in the course of human affairs been known, that military governors, set over the distant provinces of a state, have proved themselves friends to liberty, or promoters of trade? Those who expect it of them, have attended very little to the influence a prejudice contracted by education, hath over the human mind.

The man who wishes, or hopes, to make the natives of Bengal useful to Great Britain, must strictly follow your plan of increasing the consumption, and exportation of the surplus grain, and manufactures of this kingdom. The cultivator of the soil, and manufacturer of the cloth, and other articles of the export trade, are so blended and connected together, that the oppression or injury offered to one, is immediately felt by the other. On the principles on which the East India Company are founded, and the established mode by which their affairs are now under your management conducted, every good national purpose for holding these provinces, is answered. The moment you change the form of government, and

and lay the trade open, every good now accruing to the English nation, will be lost.

I know that there are many well meaning men, who think that the British empire is become too extensive and unweildy, to be longer properly governed on the principle of a simple or limited monarchy, and that the introduction of military governors into its distant provinces, is but a natural symptom of its near approach to despotism. Tho' I must own that there are many strong arguments in favour of that opinion, yet I hope that there is spirit and strength enough left in the constitution, to enable it to revert back in time to its first principles. There is not a doubt, but that too great a portion of the military spirit, hath been introduced into the management of the affairs of the East India Company abroad. The influence acquired by the ministry in Leadenhall-Street, will not lessen that spirit. An opportunity will soon offer, from the expiration of the Company's charter, to new model the form of government in these distant provinces. There are two things which must be avoided at that critical period, both of which, I much fear, the ministry will labour to effect, because they will prepare the way for the introduction of despotism, to which the princes and ministers, in all the monarchies that have ever yet appeared on the face of the earth, have had a strong propensity. I mean by taking the Company's landed possessions into the hands of government, and incorporating the India stock with the national debt, for which they will grant government security, and lay open the trade to Asia. Let any man who thinks these fears chimerical, advert to what large strides have been made by a venal House of Commons, within these last twelve years, towards furnishing the Prince with the powers of an absolute government.

Every one of the nations who have traded to Asia by the Cape of Good Hope, commenced with the true spirit of merchants, justice, equity, punctuality, and moderation. Whilst they adhered to those principles, their trade flourished, and extended over all Asia; but when, intoxicated by success, and allured by ambition, they neglected those prudent maxims, or changed them, by admitting by degrees, too great a portion of the military spirit, from that period their influence as merchants declined. The chicanery of politics, the blaze of war, and clash of arms, kept up the ball for a time, but these produced their usual fruit—oppression, poverty, slavery, and rags. Where is now the grandeur and pride of Ormus, and of Goa? Sunk even lower than that of Pondicherry and Chandernagore; and the condition of these are, God knows, miserable enough.

It must be admitted, that the nature of the British government, the spirit and genius of her people,

ple, her naval power, and peculiarly happy situation, promises a longer duration to her empire, than has hitherto happened to any preceding one which has hitherto appeared on the face of the earth. But all this will not prevent her decline, if the principles on which she was governed, in raising to such imperial greatness as she now enjoys, be neglected and forgotten. If the military spirit supplants the mercantile, in any part of her wide extending dominions, that part will first be sensible of the change: nor would any part of her vast empire decline so soon, in consequence of such a change, as her Asiatic provinces. They pay their tribute in rich merchandize. The collectors of this tribute must be trained up merchants, who must also possess the civil power, and hold the purse strings. To this power the military must be subordinate, or the whole will degenerate into tyranny, under whose baleful influence, no mercantile plant can ever flourish.

Whoever shall be minister at the termination of the old charter, if he wishes to increase the power of the crown by any possible means, without regard to the true interest of the nation, the cant will be renewed, of the impropriety there is in a company of merchants holding kingdoms in subjection, and possessing, in bar to all other of his Majesty's subjects, an exclusive right to so extensive and beneficial a branch of trade as that to Asia.

Myriads

Myriads of pamphleteers will be employed, set speeches will be made, and the great leviathan will be amused with a barrel, whilst the state projectors run away with the ship. That is, the Company's original stock, with what the minister shall please to allow them for their forts, garrisons, lands, and tenements, will be, in the language of 'Change-Alley, *consolidated*. King's officers will be sent to govern these mercantile provinces, the East India Company annihilated, and the trade laid entirely open to all his Majesty's subjects; and the solid, and almost exclusive benefits, now enjoyed by the English nation, divided amongst all the nations of the world; and all this brought about to secure the Ministry thirty additional votes in the House of Commons. This is one side of the picture; but thank God, there is yet another not so glaring perhaps, but infinitely more solid; for it hath truth, experience, and national prosperity, for its object.

THERE is not a man, the least conversant in the nature of commerce, but will admit, that it would be more for the interest of a kingdom, constituted, governed, and situated, like Great Britain, to send to Asia, a million sterling annually in bullion, and have the returns in the articles of merchandize, than to receive double the sum from these provinces in specie, by way of tribute, without any trade at all. How infinitely more advantageous will her intercourse with these provinces be, when it shall be be made to appear, that the managers of this great and important branch of national commerce, have it in their power, without fraud, rapine, or any other illegal means, to export annually to a certain fale in India, a million and a half worth of the wrought manufactures of the nation; and to make returns from Asia to the port of London, in rich articles of Asiatic merchandize, which would find ready fale in Europe, to the full and neat amount of 4,500,000*l.* sterling annually. I have as clear an idea of the manner how the above exports and imports may, with safety, ease, and honour to Great Britain, be effected, as I have of any of the most simple proposition in arithmetic; and when I sat down to write these Letters, I conceived that it was very easy to communicate the idea to you, Sir, and others, whose interest, as well as duty, it is, to know it as well as I do; but in attempting the elucidation, I have found difficulties, of which, at first, I had not the least conception. We have, in the long struggle for power, which has been kept up with various success, and with various sorts of enemies, for more than twenty years, deviated widely from our first principles. Corruptions, mismanagements, deviations, and innovations, have vitiated the original constitution of the Company. A military spirit hath grown up, and almost suppress'd the mercantile spirit; and this hath caused so great a change in the order of things, that I have frequently found, that though my postula-

tums

tums and reasoning thereon, were true, and applicable to the constitution of the Company, as a mercantile body, yet appeared chimerical, and almost ridiculous, when applied to them in their present unsettled state. They are become something more than merchants, and less than sovereign Princes. Whilst the managers at home, say that trade is their only object, their military servants abroad pant after conquests. They are precisely in that dangerous situation, where the Portugueze, the Dutch, and the French, have been before them. Security, prosperity, and duration, points back to their first principles. Ambition, avarice, and false pride, looks forward to conquest and dominion; and that will breed the worm which destroyed the grandeur and mercantile influence, of their predecessors in Asia; and if pursued, will ultimately destroy them. If, at the approaching favourable crisis, of the termination of the Company's charter, it shall please God to direct the hearts of our rulers, to grant another charter, formed and digested on the true national mercantile principles, where the military shall be totally subservient to the civil power, the commanding officer having a seat in council in military affairs only, and where the state shall reserve to themselves, a sufficient controlling power over the Company, to prevent so necessary and useful a body of men, from forming aerial schemes, of raising the dividends on the stock into a bubble, to the discredit of the nation, and

prejudice

prejudice of individuals, on the one hand; and on the other, from sinking into low, dark, designing, selfish, stock-jobbing pedlars, whose spirit and principles is as foreign from that of a candid, ingenious body of English merchants, as that of a band of banditti, is from that of a corps of brave officers. I will here risk one thought, which may probably, if made a clause of some future act of Parliament, or charter, be a check on the forementioned evils; viz. that the new Company shall divide the first year, no more than *six per cent.* the second *seven,* and the third *eight,* at which it shall continue to be fixed, and never rise higher. That all the surplus shall be formed into a stock, similar to the national sinking fund, and set apart to supply extraordinary contingencies, or be applied to make up the dividend *eight per cent.* if by losses at sea, or other unforeseen accidents, the next annual proceeds should fall short, and be insufficient for that purpose. And this surplus fund to be under the controul of Parliament.

I HAVE already said, that I used your name without your knowledge. Indeed these Letters are of such a nature, that they cannot be shewn to any one for advice. One would object to their being too bold; another, that the reasoning is too general; and a third, that it is too particular. The Directors will be angry, and perhaps order the Author home; the military will be for having
him

him tied up to the halbert; the miniſtry will laugh at him; and the critics mince his lucubrations all to all ſcraps. But you, Sir, who know him very well, and who, as I ſaid ſomewhere before, will be called upon by your Prince and country, to give your aſſiſtance in forming and digeſting a code of laws, to be inſerted in the new charter, (if one is to be granted, which, for the honour and happineſs of my native country, I hope will be the caſe,) will bear with the blunders, incorrections, and other faults, in the hope of finding ſome few mercantile ideas, which may be of uſe to you in the great national undertaking abovementioned.

THIS Letter is, by unforeſeen digreſſion, become already ſo very long, that was I now to enter into a diſcuſſion of the matters propoſed in the firſt part, it would ſwell into a book. I ſhall, therefore, cloſe it here, and endeavour, in a third, which I will take the liberty to addreſs to you, whether you continue in the government or not, to lay down a plan, for combining and fixing the national trade to Aſia in ſuch a manner, as will make it permanent, and for ever uſeful to the Engliſh nation.

LETTER III.

FROM A

FREE MERCHANT in BENGAL,

TO

WARREN HASTINGS, *Esq.*

HONOURABLE SIR;

I HAVE already addressed to you two Letters on the subject of Asiatic commerce; this is a third; and so interesting and unbounded is the subject, I cannot promise that all I have to say, will be included in this.

FROM the most early period of time, Europe has supplied Asia with silver and gold, and received in return, spices, odoriferous gums, rich silks, muslins, and coarse callicoes. The mines in Europe were wrought to supply this great drain, until the more rich ones in the New World were discovered. From that

that period, Spain imported from her American dominions, as much as was wanted for the use both of Europe and Asia. To find out the tracks the precious metals found, by which to penetrate into the interior parts of Hindoostan, would require a more minute discussion, than is necessary for my present purpose. Suffice it to say, that from the River Indus, along the coasts of Guzurat, Cambaya, and Malabar, south, to Cape Comorin, and from thence northward, along the coast of Coromandel and Orissa, to the Ganges, there are dispersed great numbers of rich trading cities, to which, both before, and since the discovery of the passage round the Cape of Good Hope, most of the trading nations of the earth, have found means to convey silver and gold, which they gave in exchange for the rich articles of merchandize, both wrought and unwrought, the produce of the great Asiatic peninsula, known by the name of India Proper.

The influence the English East India Company have acquired in this rich and extensive country, in particular on the sea coast, described in the above paragraph, is well known to every body. The Portugueze, the Dutch, and the French, have, in their turns, enjoyed great influence, and great power; but by changing their conduct, and from peaceable merchants becoming military tyrants, their influence and power have sunk to nothing, and their names have become names of reproach

over

over all Asia. On their first trading to India, the line was very judicious, and carefully drawn between the civil and military power. The last, whilst trade was the sole object of their employers, were prudently held in a state of entire dependence on the first. They traded with arms in their hands, it is true; but it was more with a view to the security of their own property, than with intention to plunder that of others. When they had, by servile adulation, and by presents to the Princes of the country, obtained a grant of a small district or territory, whereon to erect factories, they walled them round, and the troops employed to guard them, were permitted by the neighbouring Princes, or states, as things necessary to the credit of an opulent body of merchants, whom they permitted as such to reside among them. Whilst this first principle of mercantile polity was strictly adhered to, and their troops were considered as guards, or watchmen set over their merchandize, and only increased, as the factories multiplied or extended, the nation from whence they came, drew real befit from their Asiatic commerce; but no sooner was this moderate mercantile spirit vitiated by, or changed for, that of the military, from that moment did the real interest of their native country decline in India. When leaving the profession of merchants, they affected to be conquerors, and from private citizens, became sovereign Princes, blinded and led on by their passions, they left behind

hind their first principles, and the catastrophe was for ever, and at all times; inevitably the same.

A Prince of the Blood of the House of Braganza, asked an old Portugueze Admiral, what would be the best means to recover the national trade to India. " Recall four fifths of your troops, hang up " nine tenths of the priests, apply the money which " is spent in maintaining of them, to augment your " naval power," *said the old veteran;* " and the " trade will recover of itself." " I was sent," said General Lally, " to India to ruin one Company, " and have ruined two." He did not advert sufficiently to one circumstance, which was, that the English Company had not, at that time, deviated so much from mercantile principles as the French had done, or his observation would have been as applicable to the condition of the former, as it was to that of the latter. Lally's impatient military spirit, finished the work Du Plessis' ambition had begun, and totally ruined the trade of France to Asia.

The English East India Company have so far deviated from their first principles, on the coast of Coromandel, as to become military auxiliaries to a rapacious despot, instead of a respectable body of merchants, in alliance with a powerful Prince, whose country they were meant to benefit, as well as their own, by a due regulation of the tariff. The

troops

troops of the Nabob are now in arrears of pay; for as that Prince extends his dominions, his subjects are but the more oppressed; and as the military spirit increases, the mercantile spirit declines. Another war in the Carnatic, will most likely ruin both, by transferring the power to other hands. Lord Pigot saw this, and wished to prevent it, by restoring the Tanjour country to its proper Prince; but the military spirit had acquired too great an ascendency in the Council at Madrass. Those mercantile managers for the Company, had lost sight of their first profession. Instead of attending to the commercial concerns of their employers, or of their own, they had lent their money, at high interest, to the Nabob, who could not pay them, but by grievously oppressing both his old and new subjects. To enable him to do this, that they might draw from him the advantages proposed, they violently divested his Lordship of the government. If this manœuvre doth not bring after it the ruin of the Carnatic, before the Company can interpose, it will be because the French are not yet quite ready, or that Hyder Ally is accidentally, and fortunately for us, employed in subduing the Dutch settlements on the Malabar coast.

It may not be amiss to enquire here, how it has happened that the Dutch, who contributed much to drive the Portugueze out of India, have not themselves suffered the same fate from the French

or

or the English. As to the French, they, from the nature of their government, set out with too great a portion of the military spirit, and that spirit will for ever prevent them from having any very permanent commercial establishments in any part of the world, far distant from the parent state; as such establishments can only be protected by a great naval power; and a great naval power is impracticable for a monarchial state to form, and maintain for any long time, whose principle of government borders so nearly on despotism, as doth that of France. A very small portion of the mercantile spirit, was mixed up in the government of the settlements they formed in Asia. The military spirit preponderated too much, and this added to the lively capricious disposition of the nation, hurried them on to conquest and dominion, by which they were themselves ruined, before they had time to fix themselves securely, and attempt the ruin of their rivals. Besides, a Frenchman will not deign to quarrel with a Dutchman, whilst an Englishman is to be found. Had they succeeded in their attack on Madrass in the late war, the English power in India, would in consequence, have been extremely reduced, and then the Dutch would not have escaped them long. The settlements of that Republic in Asia, are precisely in the same situation as the Republic itself is in Europe; they hang suspended by a single hair. It is necessary to the balance of power, accidentally established between the leading

states

states in Europe, that the Republic should exist; and on that precarious tenor she will exist, until some two or three of the leading states on the continent, shall have settled among themselves, in what manner to share her spoils. The English, her natural friends, will interpose, and may, for a time, protract her fall: but fall she must, and that, perhaps, sooner than is generally imagined. When the Dutch covertly assist the French, to reduce the power of the English in Asia, they may be said to be infatuated, and totally blind to their real interests; for their very being as a trading state in Asia, depends on the power of the English, more than on their own. Here they are quite ripe for destruction; and but for the fortunately accidental interposition of the English power, which the commercial jealousy of the Dutch will not permit them to see, they would have been ruined long ago. Rigid virtue, severe economy, and unsullied mercantile probity, are the principles on which their state was established. How far they have adhered to their first principles, as it relates to their character as a nation, or their situation in Europe, I am not here to examine; but that they have forgot them all in Asia, I shall presently make appear. It is somewhat strange, that the people of the colonies, sent out, or planted, by a mercantile republic, as well as the subjects which they acquire by foreign conquests, have been governed on principles very different from the spirit which animated the parent state,

state, in all ages of the world; but so it is, and ever has been; and this may be proved by references to the history of the Tyrians, the Athenians, the Carthaginians, Venetians, Genoese, and Hollanders. How it comes to pass that a people, whose spirit of government is established on virtue and economy, should, on the instant they acquire foreign dominions, call in a new principle by which to manage them, and that the most dastardly to which the human mind is subject, *(fear,)* and thereby sow the seeds of their own destruction, is to me inconceiveable.* The Island of Ceylon is rich in various articles of merchandize, very extensive, and prodigious fertile; was formerly well peopled, and well cultivated; but since the total conquest of it by the Dutch in the war of 1762, when they subdued the kingdom of Candy, it

---

* The writer, when these Letters were composed in 1776, had in his mind our injudicious attempt to tax the Americans, by laws to which they had not given their assent. The consequences are too well known, and includes another instance of the folly of parent states, first permitting colonies to become numerous, and imbibe the spirit of liberty and independence, and then make attempts to enslave them. The Dutch settlers at the Cape of Good Hope, were on the point of trying their strength with their parent state, when the late war interposed, and roused the Dutch from their slumber at home; and though they may find it difficult to cause the French to withdraw their troops entirely from the Cape of Good Hope, when ever that event shall take place, they will send a sufficient number of their own, to overawe the colonists; if not, the latter will soon follow the example of America, and declare themselves independent.

wears

wears a different face. The inhabitants are reduced to nearly one half. The survivors are perfect slaves, and permitted to cultivate nothing but the cinnamon tree and pepper shrub; for the produce of which, their taskmasters allow them a most miserable pittance. Was a foreign power to land on the Island, the natives would revolt to a man. How long they would have been free from such a visit, and what would have been the consequences of it, had the French succeeded on the Coromandel coast, in the late war, I will leave them to determine. They have subdued and surrounded the Island of Java in the same manner. Here they draw their principal advantage from the industry of the Chinese. But so rigidly severe is their government, both of the native Javans and of the Chinese, and so ill affected are both those casts of people to their despotism, that was a strong squadron of ships to appear on their coast, with a force equal to that sent by the English in the late war, from Madrass to the Manillas, the Dutch would be driven from the Island in a month. The Spice Islands are held by the same tenure, and indeed, so are all their possessions to the eastward; and nothing could prevent their sinking into the same miserable insignificance with their predecessors the Portugueze, but that the English, who, though their rivals as merchants, yet that rivalry is so tempered by their friendship to them, as subjects of an European state, in friendly and strict alliance with Great Britain,

tain, that it secures to them their present possessions, in a manner more permanent, than any remaining power or influence of their own could possibly do.

England is now,* with respect to the United Provinces, as the elder sister of the same house, in possession of the sovereignty, to a younger sister by the same parents. Their political interests are the same; they must flourish or decline together. As no little squabbles about caps, ribbons, or pins, should induce a personal dislike to one another in the two natural sisters, neither should a few trifling mercantile differences in interest and opinion, induce a want of friendship in the political sisters. If they must squabble about spice and salt petre, when considered as commercial rivals, let those accidental differences in mercantile polity, be abated and adjusted on their own principles. As neighbouring states, it is their mutual interest for ever to agree, and support one another. United as maritime powers, who is it that dare attempt to give them laws with impunity? Divided, they weaken each other, to the benefit of their common enemy. The fall of the Republic will draw after it the fate of Monarchy. The fall of the Monarchy would bury the Republic with its ruins. As states they are natural friends; as merchants, I believe, from the

* This Letter was written in 1775.

nature

nature of things, they must be enemies. I wish a division of the advantages of the latter, could be so equitably made between them, as to give content to both: But this may be attempting to wash the Blackamoor white. A further acquisition of dominion in India, would involve the English in perpetual wars, and the most trifling miscarriage, enentangle them in such difficulties, as to render impossible the necessary attention to the mercantile interest, from which alone, the nation can draw any real and permanent advantages.

THE acquisition of the Island of Salset, which in a manner surrounds the Island of Bombay, is sufficient to secure the latter from the danger of a famine. A further extent of dominion on that side the Indian peninsula, would be injurious to us as a mercantile people. Any arguments which may be urged, to prove the necessity of taking in the country between Bombay and Surat, may with equal justice be enforced, for proceeding on to Cambaya, to Guzurat, to Poonah, and to Delhi. When merchants become too strongly infected with the military spirit, no line can be drawn to satisfy them. The peaceable possession of Bombay is necessary to the Company, and to the state: it is secured to them by the late cession of Salset. The influence their situation there gives them, is sufficient for every good mercantile purpose. We may, if we please, go on to lose Great Britain in Asia;

as Mr. Pitt said you won America in Germany. Swell, reptile, until you are obliged to remember the frog in the fable.

Leave the Mahrattas to settle the succession in their own government. Let which party soever prevail, they will readily grant you all you want, a fair and equitable adjustment of the tariff. You command the sea coast of Malabar with your natural arms, a marine force. Bombay is a noble magazine and arsenal; a place of retreat, refreshment, and for the repairs of your ships. The Mahratta government favours all kinds of merchants; we as such, are necessary to them: They never will know us in any other character. Send them a bale of British broad cloth as an ambassador, and they will do justice to, and respect the owners. From this fairly acquired and well chosen center, our influence extends in a glorious circle, as far as, in prudence and moderation, we can wish it. Leave conquest, and the trade of making slaves, to despots, and the slaves of despots. Firmly rooted at Bombay, and supported by the true mercantile principles, justice, equity, punctuality, and moderation. What more would we have? Even now our influence extends northward to Surat, to Cambaya, and to the River Indus, with a permanency very different from that acquired by the Macedonian freebooter, Alexander. At these places we obtain, on just and reasonable terms,

terms, innumerable sorts of stained and unstained calicoes, with which we supply Europe, Africa, and America: from Hudson's Bay to the Equator, on both sides the great Atlantic Ocean; cotton for our trade to China and Bengal; and piece goods of a thousand sorts and dyes, with which we supply the marts in the Gulf of Persia and of Mocha. From the first we bring home bullion, which lessens the necessity of the export from the parent state; and from the last, as much coffee, as suffices to fumigate the brains of all our statesmen and politicians, from John-a-Groat's house to the Land's End. To the southward, not a Prince on the Malabar coast, but respects our national flag, and supplies us with the best pepper and cardamums in the world, cheaper, and in greater abundance, than to any other people. March out of our factories of Tellicherry, Calicut, and Anjango, and attempt a conquest of the countries round about, and the natives will first resist, then despise, and at length expel us: or if we barely keep footing, as our contemporaries and rivals, the Portugueze at Goa, the French at Mahie, and the Dutch at Cochin, they will lay us under contributions, and treat us with the contempt such impolitic infatuation deserves.

From Bombay Island to the eastward, over all the Mahratta dominions, our broad cloth, copper, iron, lead, ironmongery, and hard ware, is permitted

permitted to pass from province to province, without the least obstruction, after having paid an impost of three per cent. which is but just the half of what the Company themselves charge as duty, on the importation of those articles of British manufacture at Bombay. To the west, on the other side the Indian Ocean, there is not a port on the coast of Arabia, Abyssinia, and Africa, to which we do not trade with safety; and receive from them, for the Europe and China market, assafœtida, dragons blood, verdigrease, aloes, together with olibanum, myrrh, and several other aromatic gums. What more do we want? Mistress of the seas, protectors of fair traders, and scourge of pirates. Can we, as British subjects, wish, or obtain, a more glorious or enviable situation? If more of the productions of the kingdoms and states situated on the west side of the great Asiatic peninsula, commonly called India, are wanting for our trade to any country on the west side the Cape of Good Hope, we have but to say so, and they will be provided. Where then is the use of military triumph, and useless conquests? Are not the appellations of merchants, friends, and protectors, preferable to those of freebooters, enemies, and destroyers? I pass now from the Malabar to the Coromandel coast, and in my way, cast an eye of pity and compassion, on the miserable inhabitants of the Island of Ceylon, held in a state of most grievous slavery, that the Dutch may have the sole

priviledge

priviledge of serving the rest of the world with cinnamon. It is impossible to consider the situation, extent, fertility, and numerous conveniencies of this beautiful Island, without seeing that it was intended by providence to be the mercantile mistress of the Indian Ocean. There is not an article of Asiatic merchandize, that it would not produce; hath several good ports, and one of the finest harbours in the world; but not a vessel belonging to it, but a few of the worst constructed fishing boats in the universe, in which the wretched natives are sent to fish for their inhuman tyrants. Did their masters permit those miserable beings to make their fishing craft more useful or commodious, they would serve them for the means of escape from their tyranny. They are not even permitted to approach any vessel which passes the coast, to benefit by changing their fish for sugar, rice, or any other of the necessaries of life. The haughty Republicans fix the galling yoke of slavery on the necks of a nation of inoffensive Asiatics, who never could have injured them, but would not suffer the Spanish tyrant to treat them in the same way.—Pedling monopolizers of all the spices, your measure of inequity is not yet full.

The English held on the coast of Coromandel, besides their presidency of Madras, the town of Cudalore, under the protection of Fort St. David. The French had taken the former from them, during

ring the war which commenced in the year 1743. This, with some grants they had obtained from the Subahs of the Decan, had given a spur to the military spirit, which, in its course, for ever destroys the mercantile. Madrafs had been restored by the peace of Aix-la-Chapelle; but the French, grown impatient for conquest and dominion, were become troublesome and uneasy neighbours, whose views were plainly to engross the whole of the confidence of the Princes of the country. To Mr. Orm's History of the Carnatic, I refer those who wish to see their proceedings in full detail. Preservation of their own rights, and legally obtained priviledges, first called the English to the field. It was a war of self defence, and therefore justifiable by all laws, human and divine. At the peace of Paris, the English were on the Coromandel coast, in the situation the French had been in at the peace of Aix-la-Chapelle. A restless military spirit, and total neglect of their mercantile interests, ruined the latter. I hope the former will advert to the causes of the ruin of their rivals, and benefit from it, by looking back in time to first principles. If the Company's annual balance sheet of profit and loss by their trade on the Coromandel coast, were to be closely examined, it would be found, that their gains were greater in the fifteen years which preceded the loss of Madrafs, than they have been in the fifteen years which have elapsed since the capture of Pondicherry. What good purpose then can

can it anfwer, that we go on to gratify the Nabob Mahommed Ally Cawn, in depopulating the country, in order to extend his dominions? If, with the poffeffion of two well fituated towns on the fea coaft, and the character of opulent, refponfible, and fair merchants, every good national purpofe could be effected, what end doth it anfwer, that we ftrain ourfelves to the utmoft extent of our power, at a great expence of Englifh blood and Englifh honour, to obtain, on falfe principles, what is fo eafily to be obtained on true? Let us examine the conduct, as merchants, we ought to have purfued, after the peace of Paris, and compare it with that our military phrenfy hath forced us into, and fee whether it is not proper for us to acknowledge the miftakes we have made, and correct our conduct in time, to avoid the confequences.

THE peace of Paris left us in full and entire poffeffion of all the coaft of Coromandel, except the ruins of Pondicherry. There is not a doubt, but that in the long and bloody war in the Carnatic, great injuftice had at times, been done to many of the petty Princes; nor was it until the general peace, in our power fully to adminifter juftice. We had experience enough of the defpotic principles of the Afiatic Princes. Inftead of encouraging this difpofition in the Prince we had fet up, we fhould, on principles of common equity, have
played

played them one against the other, by doing right to the whole. The surrounding Princes, feeling the effects of our impartial distribution of justice, would have been content with their own rights, and stood in awe of our power. Our own Nabob should have been made to know, that the days of misery, devastation, and oppression, were past and done away; that peace and justice were restored; that he must turn his mind to setling his country, by encouraging the arts of peace. Agriculture should have been encouraged, manufactures protected, and security insured to the lives and properties of all his subjects. Such a conduct had been easy for us to have pursued; and such conduct would have prevented the cruel ravages, different measures have since brought on the provinces by the Madura war, the invasion of Hyder Ally, and destruction of the kingdom of Tanjour, which have more than once, brought our affairs on the coast to the brink of ruin. Some individuals, no doubt, made great fortunes; and the foolish and ostentatious display they made of them on their return to their native country, gave the Ministry an itching to come in for a share. Sir John Lindsey was sent out as an Ambassador from the Crown. The Nabob, like a true eastern despot, took up the idea of playing off the King against the Company, that is, the English nation against itself. Instead of residing in the center of his dominions, and employing himself in the government of his country, on

sound

found principles, he spent his money and time, caballing and intriguing with the King's officers, and Company's servants, at Madrafs. An alarm was taken at home; and Lord Pigot, on his coming out, received instructions to find the means, by restoring the Tanjorean Prince to his dominions, and by other ways, to set some bounds to the restless, ambitious designs of the Nabob; but it was too late; the military spirit had destroyed the mercantile; and Lord Pigot, in attempting to execute his orders, was divested of his government, confined under a military guard, and the moment I am now writing, it is reported at Bengal, that the usurpers intend to send him by force on board ship, in order to his going to Europe.

Will any man deny, that on the coast of Coromandel, the English Company, or their servants, are pursuing the same steps, which heretofore brought ruin on the Portugueze and the French, and which has made the Dutch settlements ripe for destruction? The Carnatic Nabob is wily, treacherous, and revengeful. The Princes round about are dissatisfied with our conduct, and alarmed and disgusted by his power. Hyder Ally, his rival, and the enemy of every European nation, is busy in destroying the Dutch settlements in the King of Cochin's dominions; and Monsieur, at the French Islands, is not yet quite ready to take advantage of our egregious folly and misconduct. I hope no fear which my friends may feel on my account, will cause them to suppress these Letters. If I must suffer for speaking truth, let it come as it may; I am prepared for it with that invulnerable consciousness of integrity, which malice cannot reach. It wants not the classical diction of a Junius, or the well turned periods of a Johnson, to convey plain truths to the public. The soundness of the reasoning will fix the attention too close to the matter, to leave time for, or raise inclination in the sensible reader, to cavil at the incorrectness of the language. At no period of time since the last peace, hath the Company's affairs on the Coromandel coast, been in so much disorder and confusion, as they are at this juncture. The Nabob is indebted immense sums to individuals, who are scrambling for it. He is greatly in arrears of pay to his troops. The country is distressed in every province, and the Company's expences exceed their income. Discipline is relaxed; anarchy in the council; an active enemy on the coast, who will not miss the opportunity to attempt the recovery of their power; the present managers at Madrass despied, and an empty treasury. What all this will produce, is not difficult to foresee, nor easy to prevent. But as some remedy must be attempted for these growing evils, I think it impossible the great points can be mistaken. The Nabob must be sent to reside at Arcot; and restricted to correspond with Governor and Council only, not with them as individuals. His ambitious

ambitious plans and schemes of extending his dominions, counteracted, by strict and impartial justice being rendered to the surrounding Princes, who now dread his power, and doubt our honesty; the military spirit so much repressed, as to reduce it to an implicit obedience to the civil power; and the King's officers in command of the squadron, confined to the care of their own element. I will not doubt the abilities of *Sir Robert Harland*, *Sir John Lindsey*, and *Sir Edward Hughes*, to command a squadron of the King's ships, nor in this place contend, that they ever shewed the least improper attention to their own interests; but I will doubt their capacities and abilities, of entering into political intrigues with an artful eastern Prince, which can produce either honour or advantage to their King or country. That I may not be misapprehended by those great sea officers or their friends, I mean by the words *improper attention to their own interests*, a most scandalous inattention to the means used by the agent victuallers, in providing provision for the squadron, and the rates they charge them at to government. I hope this hint, however untimely introduced, may be of some use to my hardly dealt with honest countrymen, the common seamen, navigating the King's ships on duty in the Indian Ocean.

It is surprising to see what poor mercantile returns this whole coast hath ever made to the English

lish nation. A man who has read of the bloody conflicts, the sieges, the sea engagements, the loss of men, and consumption of money, that the wars with the French in the Carnatic, has cost the English nation, would naturally imagine, that immense advantages must have accrued from the peaceable possession of this whole coast, from Point Palmiras to Ceylon, for so long a term of years. To set him right, I refer him to the Company's accounts, which, after he has perused, my word for it, he will come over to my opinion, that the Company, by their present policy, are but digging a grave for the national commerce on the coast of Coromandel: And if they injudiciously permit the present growing military spirit at Bombay, to induce them to quit the Island of Salset, and plant the national colours on the continent on that side the peninsula, the whole of their possessions in Asia, will be involved in war, anarchy, and desolation.*

I AM convinced that the observation continually in the mouths of some leading men abroad, is erroneous, viz. that we have gone too far to retreat with safety, and that to secure what we have, it is absolutely necessary to conquer, or disable, every principal power on the continent, within the latitude of twenty-six degrees north, that is, from Allahabad west, to the River Indus. The more

*This was written in 1776.

northern nations will never permit this; or if they should, what good purpose will it answer? Can the parent state permit such an annual drain of her subjects, as will be necessary to hold in obedience, such an extent of dominion? Or will the possession of it increase your national trade? I believe quite the reverse. For if causes exactly similar, and in similar situations, produce the same effects, is it not natural to conclude, that in the attempt you will meet the same fate the other European nations have met before you?

In opposition to the foregoing observation, I will risk another, which, with some few exceptions, and those owing to our untoward situation in the Carnatic, will, I am persuaded, suit the national interest much better; and that is, that except in the provinces now held by the English in Bengal, the national flag should never be seen flying on the continent of India, out of sight of the sea shore; within that distance, all the merchants, and merchandizes we want, are to be found. Our intercourse with the natives, should be in the quality of merchants; whilst it is continued on that principle, it will be useful to the nation; change the principle, and the advantages are no more.

The trade to China, considered in a national view, is rather a commerce of necessity than of choice. We import her articles of luxury, to prevent our neighbours from smuggling them in upon us. As to their raw silk, I think I could make it appear, that the importation of it into England, might be lessened, or even done without. But when I come to treat of the trade to Asia in detail, as I shall consider the Company's trade to China, rather as a channel, by which a remittance may be made of the balances due from the neat proceeds of their estates in India, than in any other point of view, I shall leave it as a matter not very material to my general plan, whether raw silk be, or not, part of the returning cargoes of the China ships.

I RETURN home again to Bengal: The acquisition and peaceable possession of its provinces, properly managed, will become a great source of wealth, power, and grandeur, to Great Britain. Its barrier lines have been drawn by nature, and are now occupied by the Company. The extreme indolence, insignificance, and folly, of Mirza Amanna, the successor of the Vizier Sujah ul Dowlah, may make it necessary, in a political point of view, for us to dry nurse the ideot; and the collections in Cheet Sing's country may be useful, as it contributes to pay the troops stationed on the barrier, without sending more money from our own provinces. But was I to draw my mercantile line, it should be for ever confined within the Caramnassa. The provinces of Bengal and Bahar, and part of Orissa, contain every thing we want as a trading people;

nor

nor whilst we continue reasonable, just, and quiet neighbours, will the surrounding potentates ever dare to disturb our repose. The French may wish to do it; but whilst we continue at peace, and in friendship, with the Princes of Hindoostan, their utmost efforts must prove feeble and ineffectual. What a noble field is here prepared for a genius like that of Mr. Hastings, to exert his talents in! Away with political chicanery, despotic, or Machiavelian principles; Christian charity, justice, moderation, and mercantile probity, are all we want.

One of the ancient lawgivers, or philosophers, whose name and country I have forgot, held that citizen to be highly reprehensible, who possessed talents for public business, if he kept aloof from the service of the state. With what indignation would the old sage, if he lived in our days, view a set of men, forcing themselves into the direction of affairs of the highest importance to their country, without possessing one single qualification necessary for its proper management! If there are on the list of Directors, men so totally unfit to superintend the Company's affairs, that they know nothing of the Company's political, civil, or mercantile interest; who hardly know the names of the goods they either export or import; who are ignorant of the very complexion of the people to whose country they are sent to, or brought from; and are as well acquainted with the inhabitants of the moon, as they are

are with the power, character, interest, or connection, of the Princes of Hindooſtan, or of the geographical ſituation of the countries the Company poſſeſs; if there are, I ſay, any of that old leaven left, whoſe ignorance and ſervility, ſecured them an annual ſeat, in the deſpotic reigns of Colebrooke, Bolton, and their predeceſſors, (ſome one of whom aſked the intrepid hero Clive, whether *Sir Roger Dowlat*, as he called *Sujah ul Dowlah*, was not a *Baronet;) if there are, I repeat, let them take ſhame to themſelves, and withdraw before the day comes, when the great national queſtion ſhall be debated, whether a new charter ſhall be granted to the Eaſt India Company, or not: for I have my fears, that were thoſe *experienced men* to be examined before the Houſe of Commons, their extreme ignorance would cauſe a negative to be put on the queſtion.

I HAVE, Sir, made a moſt extravagant excurſion, but it is with intent to take a curſory view of the Company's ſettlements in India. I have done now with digreſſion, and promiſe you, in my future Letters, to keep cloſer to the original intention of them, which was to treat of the nature and conſequences of the Engliſh trade to India. If I have deviated from my plan, it was becauſe, in the pur-

---

* The ignorance of the general run of the Directors, as to the Company's political intereſt in Aſia, cannot be more ſtrongly verified, than that of a late Chairman, aſking who the NIZAM was, ſo often mentioned in the affair of Sir Thomas Rumbold.

ſuit

suit of it, I found the Company had deviated in many important instances, from their first principles. I wish to see them brought back before it is too late. The approaching period will be favourable for it. Whether you are recalled from your government, by the power of faction, or not, you must labour in laying the foundation of this great national edifice. The corner stone in the Asiatic section, must be laid in the provinces of Bengal; and who so proper to do it as yourself, who have spent the greatest and best part of your life there, in the service of your country? For the mercantile department, I will give you all the assistance I can. If I am capable of labouring at all at the pen, I will attend closely to this subject, and it shall be done in my description of the importance of the Bengal trade to the mercantile interest of Great Britain, on which I shall treat in my Fourth Letter. In the interim, I remain,

HONOURABLE SIR,

&c. &c.

LETTER IV.

LETTER IV.

FROM A

FREE MERCHANT in BENGAL,

TO

WARREN HASTINGS, *Esq.*

HONOURABLE SIR;

I am now set down to begin my Fourth Letter to you, which is to contain the first sketch of my plan for connecting the Company's trade to and from India, in such a manner, as will make it most conducive to the national interest and honour, as well as to the pecuniary advantages of the East India Company themselves.

In all commercial, as well as political concerns, constant and regular intelligence is absolutely necessary. When the Company were simply a commercial body, and had no political concerns in Asia,

the

the detaining their ships a few weeks now and then, for their letters of advice, invoices, and other mercantile documents, was sometimes unavoidable. But now they have such valuable possessions, and such interesting political concerns blended with their mercantile, it certainly is very absurd to have no regular and established modes of conveyance for their important dispatches, than by such heavy unweildy machines, as are their deep loaded merchantmen, which I have very frequently known lay ready loaded near a month, at the risk of a cargo worth, in Europe, 200,000*l.* sterling, and at a demurrage of 20*l.* per diem, waiting until the servants abroad had done wrangling, and writing minutes against one another, that the papers might be closed; and this happens every year at some, if not at all their presidencies in India. I am aware that it will be said, that the Company have their Eagle, their Mercury, and their Lapwing packets, which they dispatch on emergent occasions. I admit they have such vessels; but by some strange fatality, those vessels have been considered as mere sinecures to the captains, or machines in the hands of party. Should this be denied, I refer to the dispatches sent out on those improper vessels called packets, for seven years past, and if, on such retrospective investigation, it be not found, that they have always been used, more for the purpose of gratifying a party, than for the real use of the Company, I shall be content to be laughed at. Even this moment, we in Bengal, are gaping for the arrival of the Eagle packet, with the news of the recall of Meſſrs. Haſtings and Barwell, and the appointment of General Clavering to the government, as has been hinted in all the public and private letters by the Bengal ſhips, which left England between the months of January and May, 1776. But ſhould the miniſterial veterans in Leadenhall-Street, fail in this their attempt, I here venture to prophecy, that the Eagle will not be diſpatched at all: or if ſhe be, the papers ſhe will bring, will be duplicates, or ſome unmeaning new orders, ſent juſt to ſave appearances. Is it not to be lamented, that the paſſions and prejudices of whole bodies of men, as well as thoſe of individuals, are to be managed, and brought over to act ſuch mean and ſervile parts, even in affairs of a public nature, and of the utmoſt importance, entruſted to their care, as well as in their own private concerns?

That the Company's, and national concerns in Aſia, is of ſufficient conſequence for them to be at the expence of eſtabliſhing a regular correſpondence, will not be controverted; and I, who, on national principles, am an advocate for conducting this trade by means of a company ſimilar to that now exiſting, muſt admit, that the expence of ſuch correſpondence ſhould be borne by the Company. I therefore think, that a ſufficient number of frigates ſhould be built, each mounting twenty guns, and

and of such construction, as to insure their being prime sailers; and that one of these frigates should sail from Plymouth, or some other convenient port in the Channel, every three months, with all advices of importance; that is to say, on the following days; the first of January, April, July, and October; and this in times of peace constantly, and without the least deviation. By these regular packets, all papers, political, military, and judicial, might be sent, as well as duplicates of mercantile ones; and let the mere merchant ships proceed out and home, as soon as they are loaded, with their own documents. The only material objection to this, would be the expence of keeping eight such vessels as mentioned above, in constant pay, for this particular purpose. To obviate that, I boldly affirm, that was all the money paid by the Company for these ten years past, for the demurrage of their ships, arising entirely from their detention on account of public papers, and the sum total divided into ten equal shares, one of those shares would amount to more, than would answer the expence of eight such packet boats annually. But there are many other solid reasons for such an establishment, which must, without my assistance, occur to every man, who is possessed with the necessary abilities to qualify him for being elected into the direction, to superintend the Company's political and commercial affairs.

The packets which may be dispatched in January and April, would pass the Cape of Good Hope in time to go what is called the inward passage to India, and might be ordered to land the papers for Bombay at Anjango, then proceed to Madrass and Bengal. The first of these would return again to Madrass, to sail from thence on the first of October for Europe; the second in January; and so on in continual rotation. As some one of the ports in the Channel, should be the place from whence the packet should regularly sail every three months from Europe to India, so should Madrass be the place from whence the packet should sail from India to Europe, with regular dispatches from all the presidencies. The time for the packets to leave Europe for India, and India for Europe, I have fixed to the same days, as it suits extremely well with the seasons of the year. It will seldom happen that more than two will be at the same time on their passage out or home; so that there will be at all times one, and mostly two, of these vessels in Europe, as well as in India, preparing to take their tour out or home. Nor should their time of sailing be altered on any account, as the Company's servants at the different factories, would be sure to find a vessel at the stated time, ready to carry home their dispatches. There could be no kind of excuse for their omitting to send by them, a clear and concise statement of the Company's affairs under their management.

BESIDES

BESIDES the demurrage on the large ships mentioned above, the great charge which the Company are frequently put to, by their servants sending vessels from Bombay to Bussorah with packets, will also be saved. To this may be added a general postage on all letters out and home, should that be thought expedient. But my plan has its foundation in matters of more consequence, than a regulation of postage. If the political and commercial interests of the Company in Asia, will not bear the charge of a regular correspondence, I know not what will. The necessity and utility of the measure must strike at once, and render all arguments to the contrary insignificant, which shall be grounded on a false and pedling economy.

I am not unaware, that such a regular and methodical establishment, would often, in time of war, from necessity, be broken in upon; but this doth not make it the less useful: and for advices from Europe to India, there is another channel, which, though it was not discovered in your government, yet has by your means been re-explored, and its utility well ascertained; I mean by the Arabian Gulf and Red Sea. In no period of time, hath there been an instance of such amazing dispatch, in the conveyance of advice from one part of the world to another, as what has happened here. A letter dated in London the 24th of May, 1776, was received at Calcutta, in Bengal, on the 14th day

day of August following. Its rout was from London to Marseilles, to Alexandria, to Cairo, to Suez, and Bengal. In war time, the French, and other powers on the continent, may give some interruption to the progress of advices over land; but what power can interrupt your passage by sea? A frigate with advices from London to Alexandria, will meet with no other impediments in her passage, than what she might meet with going to port Mahon. The Company's marine force at Bombay, commands the Red Sea. And though the necessary delay, caused by the established quarantine, would impede your advices from India to Europe, it would not be the case with those from Europe to Asia.

Was I here to enter into a minute detail of the times and seasons, in which it would be proper to order vessels on such service, or to name the places where to fix agents, to conduct this part of the plan of correspondence, it would lead me much out of my way. Many, and great inconveniencies, have arisen heretofore, for want of such establishment. It is easy to prevent them from happening again, when ever the narrow, confined, pedling, 'Change-Alley principle of conducting the Company's affairs, shall be entirely expelled the heads and hearts of the managers in Leadenhall-Street.

I will explain myself, to prevent the present Court of Directors from imagining I mean them. That is impossible; for I have read the late Act of Parliament, for regulating the East India Company's affairs; since the passing of which, the secreting, or keeping private, good or bad advices from India, until stock could be bought in or sold out, will not now answer the purpose; and men will always do their duty, when there is no temptation to the contrary. When I shall take occasion to mention any vile act of selfish mismanagement, which betrays a breach of trust, or ignominious prostitution of commercial probity, such as the above noted, formerly well known practice, I hope the Proprietors, Directors, &c. will understand it as alluding to things past, and not at all applicable to present men, or present measures. Or if by accident, I should touch a sore part (for long habit is a kind of second nature) they have only to omit the practice in future, and all will go well. I own I want to see this great branch of national commerce, conducted on the most noble principles of national utility, and national honour. There is no use for 'change-broker cunning. All that will be necessary for us in future, in the conducting of the Company's affairs, is common sense and common honesty. If these virtues are not to be found among twenty-four properly chosen mercantile managers, in charge of the Company's affairs, it is not easy to say where they are to be found. I believe

lieve the manner in which the Company now freight their ships, for the purpose of carrying on their trade to Asia, is liable to as many objections, as any mode which can possibly be devised. There is also, some objections to the disposal of them. A ruling man shall procure a son, a nephew, or servile dependant, any voyage he chooses. This is an unfair influence, and in its consequences, hurtful to the service: It is preferring the interest of individuals to the common good, which a Director is sworn not to do. The remedy is at hand, equitable and easy. The homeward bound ships take their turn for being taken again into the service, from the date of their arrival at St. Helena; at which Island all the Company's ships touch, in their way home from every part of Asia. Why not let the owners of those ships choose the voyage for their ship, as it comes to their turn? Or the captains of the ships taken up in one year, or at one time, draw lots for their respective voyages? This would obviate many inconveniencies, which arise from the present partial mode. In its proper place, I will consider whether it would not be more for the interest of the Company, to allow annual salaries to their captains and officers, in lieu of private trade; and these to be increased in proportion to the rank in the service, &c. Their present mode of pretending to restrict private trade, by test oaths, and venal officers, causes a great and useless consumption of the national morality.

In order to keep up their interest, Colebrooke, and other despots of the times, preceding the year 1774, permitted more ships to be built and freighted, by one third, than were wanting for the service. They run the Company in debt to the government, the bank, and the freight owners; imported more tea than Europe could drink, or America drown; and then piously laid all the blame on their servants abroad.

In order to reduce the surplus tonnage, the state limited the Directors to a certain number of ships. The officers were put out of employment, and the captains, without being invalids, became pensioners on the Company. Thus were violent remedies become necessary to correct abuses, which men, void of public spirit, had selfishly introduced into the management of the Company's affairs.

I HAVE said in a former Letter, that one million and a half of the manufactures of the mother country, may be annually, and with great advantage, sent to the East Indies; and that the returns arising from the sales of the outward bound cargoes, together with the neat proceeds of the Company's estates in India, would be sufficient to supply returns in the rich merchandize of Asia, that should produce, free of all kinds of expences, 4,500,000*l.* in Europe. It is impossible to explain this, but by regular statements of the invoices and account sales, of the cargoes both out and home. I shall, therefore, arrange them in proper order, either at the end of this Letter, or in a number by itself; and to that I refer the reader for the proof of my assertions.

The Company's apparent necessary expences, for conducting their affairs in Europe, are very moderate; but from the partial, or injudicious arrangement of their ships, they, in many instances, are at great expences, which are altogether useless, and every year amount to immense sums of money.

The first instance of partiality, or inattention, I shall mention, is the management of what is called their Bombay and Mocha ship. This ship, from the time she is first taken into the service to carry goods to Bombay, and load home from Mocha with a cargo of coffee, to the time she is discharged, consumes full two years. Add to this another year, which, by the custom of the service, elapses before she can be again employed. How then can the owners let the ship to freight on reasonable terms, without being losers by the bargain? The truth of the matter is, the Captain's interest supersedes the Company's; and in order that he may gain five thousand pounds, the Company are put to the expence of twenty. For the ship employs three years in effecting what ought to be done in eighteen months, as will appear by the following simple detail of the fact.

The

The ships for the year, are generally nominated in the month of July, and their destination fixed. The owners set about to prepare them; and in the month of February or March following, the Bombay and Mocha ship sets sail, and generally arrives at Bombay in the month of August. Here the Captain (for he is always a favourite) is permitted to idle away his time for three or four months. The amount of his private adventure, often exceeds the amount invoice of the Company's goods sent on the same ship. It is seldom less than ten, and often more than thirty thousand pounds. If he gets his own business done sooner than it is necessary for him to go to Surat, in his way to Mocha, he is indulged with a voyage to the Malabar coast, under pretence of bringing up some of the Company's pepper, which, by the bye, ought to be left on the coast, and taken at once on board, by the ships homeward bound. But this man, say the Governor and Council, is in great favour with the leading Directors, and must be served. He will make two or three thousand pounds by the trip, and be time enough for Mocha. On his return from the coast, he is sent to Surat, where the ship takes in some trifling quantity of goods on the Company's account, and is filled up with the Captain's, or freight which goes on board, under the denomination of the Captain's private trade, and on the security of which, he lends his money at a high premium, payable at Mocha. On his arrival there, a

factory

factory is opened with great pomp and parade, and a table kept for three Supercargoes, who have been sent out of Europe, or appointed from Bombay.—To do what? Why really nothing: For the Company's Hindoo Broker provides the coffee. The Captain and Supercargoes, who, in this voyage, are always joint traders, before they leave Bombay, obtain permission to use their own money to pay for the coffee, and draw bills, at high exchange, in their own favour, on the presidency at Bombay, to which place they return in the month of August, ready loaded for Europe; but do not quit Bombay until November, and generally arrive at home in May; and by the month of July, the ship is delivered back to her owners; nor will it come in time for her to be taken up until the following season—And this is called management! In the space of three years, this ship is once completely loaded for the Company, and that is homeward bound with coffee, because the freight is paid on the returning cargo, and that saves the owners, who never concern themselves whether the Captain or Company have the use of the ship out, or whilst she is abroad. From the first to the last of this branch of the Company's commerce, there is a most notorious sacrifice made of the public interest to that of individuals. Indeed it runs so completely through the whole of the management of the Company's affairs in Europe, that I am almost sick with the thoughts of the numberless instances I shall be obliged to produce in

these

these Letters. Such an exposition of notorious mal-administration, brought home in so great a variety of instances, looks like invective, or even defamation; and I expect to be outlawed, proscribed, and even burnt in effigy, for daring to utter such biting truths, which cannot be evaded, or denied, as they are to be found in every page of the Company's records. Whilst you, the Captains, Owners, Ships Husbands, Proprietors, and Directors, look there for them, I will go on to tell you how, in justice to your employers, and to the state, you ought to manage the coffee trade.

A SHIP load in two years, is, I think, all you want for national consumption. How it happens that it costs you so much, that you cannot sell at a price low enough to induce re-exportation, may be discovered by a careful attention to the facts related in the foregoing paragraphs; nor will you be able to gain any thing by this trade on your present plan: but as half a cargo, or two thousand bales of Mocha coffee, imported annually, is all that we want at present, let us see what a difference it will make to us, when it is imported at less than half the present expence.

IT matters very little, whether we keep one of the Bombay servants as an agent at Mocha, or not, as far as it relates to the procuring of a cargo of coffee; for the Hindoo, who is the Company's

Broker,

Broker, and under whose protection he resides among a nation of bigotted Mahometans, in great credit, ease, and grandeur, will, as now, with the Captain and Supercargoes, in fact, transact the business.

The country ships which trade from Surat and Bombay, to Mocha and Juddah, carry very rich cargoes, consisting of grain, piece goods, spice, and sugar. There are in Arabia, very few articles of merchandize, with which they can load home to advantage, so that they generally return in ballast. The owners of these ships, will very readily supply your agent at Mocha with money, for bills at par, to save the risk, and bring over on freight to Bombay, as much coffee as you want, on the most moderate terms. I insist on it, that the government of Bombay, may contract with very responsible people, to supply the money at Mocha, and bring over the coffee annually, at less expence than it now costs the Company, for factory charges, and Supercargoes table expences, and have it ready at Bombay in the month of September. Your coffee ship, which arrives there in August, may return to Europe in the November following, with as much coffee as you want, and complete her cargo with Surat piece goods. In this manner the same ship will make two complete voyages to Bombay, in the space of time which is now selfishly consumed in effecting one.

Nothing

Nothing can be more irksome than I find this part of my plan. The Company will want to conduct their trade, about twenty-four ships annually, exclusive of the packets above mentioned. In arranging of these ships, and pointing out the proper time for their sailing, &c. I am inevitably led into a close investigation of the present conduct, in order to contrast it with my proposed alterations, and in so doing, such scenes of selfish iniquity must be laid open, as will rouse almost every man concerned, or employed, in the Company's service in Europe, against me. I have but two inducements to write on this subject at all: The first is a most sincere love of my country, which makes me wish to see her trade to Asia properly conducted: The second may not be altogether so justifiable, but it arises out of the first. I cannot examine to the bottom of the mean, selfish, interested views of the managers at home, without recollecting, that those very men are many of them the same who raised such a clamour against the Company's servants abroad, and to cover their own iniquity, cried out thief first. I shall, in the investigation now in hand, prove, that in no part of the service, has there been such mal-practices, as what continues yet in use, in the conduct of their shipping; to say nothing of their dextrous management of contracts. Let those gentlemen suspend their anger, until they have refuted the charges brought against them, or have altered their conduct, then I shall

be

be nothing averse to the meeting their indignation. When they shall begin, as I have pointed out the way, and either import the coffee the Company want, at half the present expence, or make it clear to the nation, that it cannot be done, I will thank them for the first, or ask their pardon if they prove the last. But until one or other happens, I shall go on to shew the ill effects of their management to the national interest, and national honour, without regarding whose ears it may chance to tingle.

Besides the ship for Bombay and Mocha, there are generally four others taken up at the same time, for the trade to that side of India. Two of these most commonly return home again directly, with piece goods and pepper. The other two are always commanded by favourites, to whose private interest the Company is for ever sacrificed. The first of these is called the Bombay and China ship, and is managed on the same principle with the coffee trade. The Captain loads out an immense cargo on his own private account, in defiance of Company's officers, whom they bribe, and of test oaths, which custom hath taught them to take with horrid indifference. From Bombay they carry to China, six hundred bales of cotton on account of the Company, which, by some subtle evasion, they call the Company's tonnage, and eight hundred bales on account of the Captain, and this constantly, and without the least variation, except that in some of

the

the large ships, the Captain's share is ten sixteenths of the whole tonnage of the ship, for which he pays not a farthing. Here *Mandeville*'s maxim of *private vices public benefits*, is *reversed*, and *public vices become private benefits*. For the Captain gains all the profits arising from such iniquitous proceedings; and this is known to the Directors, Owners, Husbands, &c. for a number of them have been Captains, and made their fortunes in the same way. A great man about Leadenhall-Street, whose name may remain snug if he so pleases, as not to wince, and thereby shew the sore place, was once on a committee of enquiry, on an accusation brought against a Captain from Bombay, for selling military stores to the country powers. This man, high in the direction, forgetting his own old practices, ironically asked his brother in iniquity, "*What he had* "*gained by the sale of his great guns?*" The Captain, who well knew that the inquisitor had done the same thing at the same place, answered more truly than wisely, "*Really, Mr. Chairman, not so* "*much as you did on yours by fifteen per cent.*" This ill timed repartee lost him the command of his ship for some time; but long usage had so blunted the feelings of those honourable despots, that in a year or two, the Captain recovered his ship, and has since made a fortune *very honestly*, I make no doubt.

There can be no honest reason assigned, for continuing of this expensive custom, of sending a ship by Bombay to China. The voyage from London to China, and home direct, is a voyage of twenty months; by Bombay, it is commonly from thirty-two to thirty-six months. What she carries from Europe to Bombay, may very fairly be put on the Bombay ships, without overloading of them. And no one will say it is for the Company's interest, to send a ship such a rout, to carry six hundred bales of cotton to China. But I shall set this matter in a much clearer light, when I come to that part of the plan, in which I propose that the Company's treasury at China, shall be supplied by the proceeds of goods from their settlements in India; and that their annual China fleet shall serve as convoy homeward bound, to all the ships from Asia in time of war.

The Bombay and Bengal ship, is governed so exactly on the same principles of the Mocha and China ones, that it would be but repeating the same words, to take further notice of her. I will confine myself to one more instance out of a dozen, where expensive, dangerous, and unnecessary voyages, are pursued purely to serve the Captain, and which, in their consequences, are highly pernicious to the interest of the nation and the Company.

The presidency at Madrass, have every year ready a cargo of goods for Europe, which they dispatch in the month of October. The ship destined to carry home these goods, arrives on the coast in June or July. Would not any man imagine, that this ship came fully loaded from Europe, with goods, military and marine stores, for Madrass only, and that she would be unloaded immediately, and reloaded, so as to quit the coast early in October, in order to avoid those dreadful gales, which are always to be expected on this coast, towards the end of that month, when the south-west monsoon gives place to the north-east, to the violence of which this whole coast is extremely exposed?—No such thing.—The Captain's interest for ever interposes, in gross violation of common honesty and common sense. It is managed at home, that this ship shall have some few stores for Bengal; and this justifies the rulers at that presidency, to understand the hints from home in the Captain's favour, and they let her proceed. This gives him the opportunity to load the ship with salt on his own account, with which he proceeds to the Ganges, on the very height of the south-west monsoon. His stay cannot be long, for he must beat back against the monsoon, to be in time on the coast to sell his returning cargo of rice, which is also his own, and take in his cargo for Europe. This obliges him to work his people night and day, in that inclement season, and most unwholesome time of the year; the consequence

sequence of which is, that half of them die with fevers and bloody fluxes, and the rest are so reduced, as scarce to be able to work the ship to the coast. Since I have been in India, no less than five of these ships have been lost, either in going down to Bengal, working back at so improper a season, or by the monsoon overtaking them before they were ready to quit the coast. When had they continued at Madrass, the peoples lives would have been saved, and the ship would have left the coast in due season, with a rich undamaged cargo for Europe.

LET us see what is the advantage the Company is supposed to draw by her proceeding on to Bengal. Why first she has some stores for that presidency, which must be sent down. I will not stoop to a controversy with a paltry clerk at the India House, to point out for what sinister motives, a ship intended for Madrass only, came to have goods on board for Bengal, because I know the thing will say, as she was taken up for Coast and Bay, she must proceed to the Bay.—Let his masters blush for abusing their employers, and the nation in general, with such unmeaning jargon, and in future, take away the plea for such unjustifiable proceedings, and freight the ship for Madrass only. But I will admit that it may happen now and then, that the Madrass October ship may have stores, or goods, on board for Bengal. Do not all the Bengal ships, deliver troops, goods, and stores, at Madrass?

Are

Are they not there on their way to Bengal at the same time? And cannot the stores, if by accident the Madrafs ship has any for Bengal, be sent on board them? Yes, they may—But then the ship wants her salt petre for ballast, and must go to Bengal for it.—I answer, the more shame for the managers—Why is it not ready at Madrafs? Every year the presidency at Bengal, send round to Bombay, several thousand bags of salt petre, to ballast home the ships from that presidency: can they not do the same to Madrafs, which lays not one third of the distance from them? I answer the question myself; they can, with great ease, and at little expence. But if they do it without orders, some favourite Captains will lose the opportunity of loading the ship down to the Bay, with salt, and back to Madrafs with rice, for his own emolument; which hath hitherto been a sufficient reason for risking the Owner's ship, Company's cargo, and the lives of the crew. The facts I here relate, and those I shall relate, are so notorious, that I will wager my life to a golden pippin, if my friend will but cause these Letters to be published, the managers will never dare to permit them in future;* in which case, I shall be the cause of saving some hundred thousands of pounds to the public, and

---

*Here the author was a little mistaken: favourite Captains continue to exist; and ships are directed to be sent certain voyages, to serve them as heretofore.

the

the lives of many of my worthy countrymen, the common tars; which last consideration is of so refreshing a nature, that, without possessing sixpence in the world, I feel myself out of the reach of, and looking down on the whole tribe of ignorant, selfish managers, that have reigned despotically in Leadenhall-Street, from the days of Child, to those of Colebrooke.

LET no man, after this, fall into the mistake which I have done, and promise to conclude his lucubrations in one or two Letters, when he proposes to treat on so unbounded a science as commerce; for if he knows any thing at all of the subject, new thoughts will arise, and new matter fall in, that will lead him often into unavoidable digression. I now plainly perceive, that to treat the subject of national commerce to Asia, in the detail I propose, of examining into every branch of the Company's management in Europe and in Asia, will require much more room, than I at first imagined.

WHEN I had written so far, I had occasion to ask a gentleman, if he remembered in what year the English first traded to Bengal. He referred me to the History of the East and West Indies, lately translated from the French by J. Justamond. I procured the work, and was so struck with the great abilities of the author, on perusing the two

first

first books of his first volume, as they are translated by Justamond, that had it been in my power to have recalled my first Letter, which had gone to Europe on the ship Triton, Captain Elphinstone, or my second and third, which I had forwarded on the London, Captain Webb, I really believe I should have committed the whole to the flames, as a very flamy piece of business. But they were gone past recall, and I entered on the perusal of his third book, which treats of the first rise and progress of the English trade to Asia, with such high expectations of finding every thing said, which possibly could be said on the subject, that I concluded, it would put an end for ever, to my having further thoughts of writing on a subject, already so copiously treated by so able a penman. Since I have read that book, I have again altered my opinion; as I have thereby found, that a man who takes all his facts from the relation of others, is very often mistaken in his premises. The Author of the History of the East and West Indies, is undoubtedly a great genius, and of unbounded historical knowledge. He has collected his materials, and wrought them up, in a very pleasing and masterly manner. But if he has been as ill informed in what he relates in the other parts of his history, as he has in that which pertains to the progress of the English in Asia, for the last twenty-five years, however harmonious his language, or however pleasing his manner, I do from my own knowledge declare, that his history,

tory, in that part, ought not to be received, or considered in any other point of view, than that of being a most beautiful historical novel, where, with a few acknowledged facts for a foundation, the author has, by the assistance of great learning, a fine imagination, and uncommon power over words, blended truth and falshood together in so bewitching a manner, as to give him a chance of misleading posterity to the latest period of time. On such foundations do your mere men of letters mount up to immortality! There is an harshness and commonality in treating of plain matters of fact, or simple truth founded on experience, particularly when they are handled by an unlettered merchant; that a work drawn up by such a genius as that possessed by the Author of the History of the Indies, will for ever have the preference with two large tribes of readers; those of great learning and universal reading, who judge of the works of an author by his diction, without regard to truth; and those who, from want of learning and abilities to read, or think at all, are extremely prone to believe the most malicious reports against their countrymen, though propagated by a declared enemy to the glory and prosperity of their nation. But there is a third order of men endued with common sense, who read and think enough, to distinguish truth from fiction, however poorly attired the former, or gaudily decked out the latter. To these I address what I have to say, in answer to the

Abbé's

Abbé's account of the progress of the English East India Company's affairs in India, since the year 1750. So long have I been an eye witness to the transactions in Asia: And though the Abbé hath every advantage over me, which a great genius, and a great scholar, can have over a plain unlettered man, yet I find not the least diffidence or fear, in entering the lists with him, on the subjects which have happened within the period above mentioned. To his superior abilities, I shall oppose a relation of the facts as they really have happened, in the plain simple garb of truth, and leave cavilling to word catchers and feeders on syllables.

The Abbé's genius hurries him on with such rapidity, that I own, in the multitude of well arranged words, I am at a loss for his meaning. He tickles my fancy, but quite confounds my understanding. He flies about from state to state, and mingles an account of nations who have been, with those who now are, in such a laconic and dogmatical stile, that the sum total of the history of many great trading nations, are summed up in a short paragraph or two, consisting of a few round assertions, often unintelligible, and oftener void of truth.

In his account of the Maldivia Islands, he is right, in saying they produce no articles of merchandize, except cowries, coir, and fish; that the
King

King resides at one of the Islands called Mole, &c. But when he adds that he is a tyrant, and the only merchant in his dominions, he is totally mistaken. The King of the Maldivias is a limited monarch, reigning over a great number of Islands. He appoints the governors to the different divisions, which, as the Abbé says, are called Attalons. Each division is taxed with furnishing a certain quantity of cowries, coir, and fish, to pay the unavoidable expences of the government; for they have no kind of money current with them. Every family pays a small part of this to the governors, after which, all the cowries they find, fish they catch, or coir they make, is entirely their own, and they dispose of it as they please. If they export it on their own account, the King, as supreme magistrate, draws a duty of three per cent. for the purposes of government; and five per cent. on all the goods his own subjects import, for the same reason. Where doth there exist a mercantile state, in which something similar is not established, to defray the expences of government? In every other respect, the natives of the Maldivia Islands, are as secure in their persons and properties, as any people in Europe. The judicial authority is in the hands of the Priests, and so equitably is it used, that there is not an instance of a native of these Islands, who navigate their trading vessels to every part of India, running away, or even staying behind, except left as agents at the port to which they

they trade. As they have no rice, or other grain, of their own growth, when the public magazines or granaries are not full, the King hath the preference given him to purchase for the public good, and he pays for it with coir and cowries, which are collected as duties. So far, and no farther, is the King of the Maldivias a tyrant, and a merchant. But it would require a work as voluminous as the Abbé's own, to refute all his wrong assertions.

The Abbé, in his account of the trade to Mocha, asserts, that the French and English used now, a cheaper method than formerly, in procuring their coffee to be brought by private ships, to their settlements of Bombay and Pondicherry. The method is certainly a good one, and may be true as to the French; but hitherto, the English Company have continued the old mode, of sending their own ships, and for no other reason than that which I have assigned in the foregoing part of this Letter, which was written before I had seen the Abbé's works; nor shall I alter it. No writer of history ever hath been more imposed upon, than the author seems to have been, from the account he gives of the expulsion of the Dutch from Bussorah, during the management of the Baron Knyphausen. It is very possible, that the Abbé may have had his account from the Baron himself, since his return to Europe. It is, however, false in every part. I will

will here give a slight, but faithful sketch, of the Baron's history, before his first arrival, and during his stay in the Dutch service in India. I know the man, and the principles on which he acted, much better than the Abbé doth; or he would never have given to the present age, and to posterity, so very erroneous an account of the reasons which caused the expulsion of the Dutch from Bussorah.

The Abbé's Baron Knyphausen, is the elder brother to the Ambassador of that name, who resided so long, in a public character from the King of Prussia, at the court of London. He was a subject of, and Lieutenant in the King of Prussia's service, and present at the action, which the army of that Prince had with the Austrians, commanded by Prince Charles of Lorrain, some time about the years 1742 or 1743. It was, I have heard, the first battle the King had ever seen. Some part of his army was broke, and very roughly handled by the Austrians. The King, who did not, it seems, command his army that day, terrified by the confusion and slaughter which surrounded him, took fright, and made a very un-soldier-like retreat; and was five leagues from the scene of action, when his General, who commanded, recalled him, with the news of his enemies having been entirely routed. This unseemly behaviour in the Prince, so roused the indignation of our young Baron, that he wrote a severe satire on his master; which coming to the knowledge

knowledge of the latter, he sent to seize the Baron, and had him closely confined. The young soldier seeing the danger he was in, found means to induce the centinel, who had him in charge, to go off with him. During several days, he and his friend the centinel, past through many dangers, by land and by water, but at length, got into the territory of the States General. Despairing of a pardon, and restoration to his honours and estate, both of which the King had transferred to his younger brother, the above mentioned Ambassador, he took employment in the Dutch East India Company's service; and was by them sent out very strongly recommended to the General of Batavia, who had some knowledge of the Baron's family. Here he remained some time, in various employments; saw his friend the centinel, made an Ensign; and having acquired a competent knowledge of merchandize, he was thought a proper person to be sent in charge of the company's concerns at Bussorah.—Very likely my intelligence hitherto, may have come from the same quarter as the Abbé's, and be equally false; for I had it from the Baron himself; not in private conversation, but in very large and public companies; where, in an ostentatious display of his own great power and abilities, he constantly convinced his audience, that whatever might be his character as a merchant, as a politician, he was entirely free from the shackles imposed by virtue, christianity, and morality.

It was a maxim with the Baron, that the Dutch and English factory flags should never fly in sight of each other. But the English were not the rivals of the Dutch at Bussorah. The former had neither sugar nor spice to vend there; the latter brought very little else. The Baron's story has been made up since his expulsion: And the Dutch at Batavia, have their ears ever open to believe any disadvantageous story of their rivals in trade. The Baron, who used truth or falshood in his narratives, as best suited his purpose, laid the blame of the treatment he received from the Turkish government, entirely to the account of the English; as much with a view of rousing the jealousy of the government at Batavia, in order thereby to obtain a force, to execute a plan he had before formed, as with intent to cover the real cause of his expulsion. The truth is this; the Baron was a man of great intrigue, and had a very high opinion of his own abilities in the service of the fair. His vanity often prompted him to boast of favours he never received. It is not easy for a European, and a Christian, in so conspicuous a station, as that in which the Baron acted at Bussorah, to negociate for himself, in affairs which lead to an intimate intercourse with Mahometan ladies. The law positively forbids such commerce, even with the meanest of the people, and a discovery is very fatal to both parties. Knyphausen's ambition led him to seek an intimacy with Duchesses and Lady Marys; and the pimps of Bussorah, like their

their brethren in all other parts of the world, promise Junos, though they deal in clouds. One of those honest men taught the Baron to believe, that the young spouse of a rich old Turkish merchant, sighed for his embraces. Secret passages, trap doors, and every other apparatus of intrigue, was prepared at the Dutch factory. Hush money was in golden showers advanced; and a trained goddess from the public stews, was conducted with great mystery to the Baron's arms. The art of the well taught courtezan, her fine cloaths, which had been procured by the Baron's bounty, together with his ignorance in the Turkish and Arabian languages, enabled the pimp and drab to impose on him for some time. But nothing could secure him from the effects of his own absurd vanity. He puffed of his success so often, and so publicly, that the Cadies Officers got intelligence of the intrigue. The factory was surrounded, and the happy pair taken together. The Baron was confined, the Lady drummed with ignominy round the town, and the Pimp lost his nose and ears. I have several times since seen the miserable mutilated wretch, imploring charity from the passengers in the public way.

WHETHER the Baron received a *bambooing* or not, I really do not remember; but I know that the English Resident, interested himself extremely with the government, to prevent so disgraceful and painful an application, to the feet of a national Resident,

Resident. Be that as it may, it cost the Baron large sums to make the matter up, and obtain his release. He was, however, at length discharged; went to Batavia; and had art enough to procure some ships of force, with which he returned to the Gulf of Persia; landed on the Island of Carrack, and sent his ships to block up the entrance to Bussorah River; laid the government under contribution, as well as the foreign merchants; and for a time interrupted the trade of the port; and obtained repayment of the money which had been forced from him, with large premium.

AFTER the death of Thomas Kouli Khan, or Nadir Shaw, the kingdom of Persia fell into great disorder. The governors of distant provinces set up for themselves, and became independent Princes. At that time, an officer named Sheik Abdulla, was in command of the strong fortress of Bundarick. It lies on the sea coast of Persia, and about six leagues north-east from the Island of Carrack, which our Baron now occupied. From the death of Nadir Shaw, to the time we are now speaking, Abdulla had kept possession of the fort, and adjacent country, more by a strict application to the advantages of commerce, which his favourable situation gave him, than by the power of his arms. The port was the most secure in all the kingdom for small vessels: Nor was the road for large ones a bad one, except when the north-west winds prevailed, and the great ships usually lay under the

small

small Island of Koulle, about four leagues distant. The road by land to Sharass, then the second city in, and now the capital of the kingdom, was open and good. Every encouragement was given to the ships and vessels of all nations, to trade to the port. The English had a factory in the town; and the Baron agreed to pay a small sum annually, as a quit rent for the Island he had previously obtained permission to seize.

No sooner had the Baron built a fort on the Island of Carrack, than he began to intrigue. Unluckily the old Sheik of Bundarick, had a young son of a most diabolical disposition; as void of the feelings of humanity, as he was of filial piety and fear. With this young desperado, the Baron kept up a friendly intercourse. If Baron Knyphausen did not approve of the young man's principles, his vanity frequently induced him to belie his own; for nothing was more common with him than to declare, that a man with the spirit, and in the situation of Mirmahana, who saw a kingdom open to his ambition, did right to seize it. The infamous parricide destroyed his father, mother, uncle, and elder brother; drove out the English, and granted an exclusive right of the trade of the port, to his friend the Baron. The Abbé is right, when he says the Baron's successors possessed not his abilities. From the character drawn of Mirmahana, by his friend Knyphausen, the following Dutch governors placed a confidence in the usurper,

usurper, which he did not deserve. He took an opportunity to surprize the fort, put the garrison to the sword, and drove the Dutch entirely out of the Gulf, to which they have never traded since. Such were the services rendered by the renegado Baron to his protectors the Dutch—And so untrue is the Abbé's account of that transaction.

It is impossible for a man, who knows any thing of the true history of the nations inhabiting the coasts of Malabar and Coromandel, to read with patience, the Abbé's account of them. He seems to me, to have been at the trouble, to have collected all the true, and all the fabulous accounts, which have ever been given to the world, of those famous countries, and to have jumbled them together in such a manner, as to render it impossible for the reader to draw any real information or knowledge from his work. Now and then, for a paragraph or two, he appears to be serious; and you begin to hope that the mercurial spirit of the Frenchman is fixed, and that he is on the point to give you a sober and rational account of some country, people, or manufacture; but in an instant he is gone, and you find your chain of reflection broke, by being hurried away you know not how, and reading a short account of some drug or mineral, when you are thinking of a piece of cotton cloth or muslin. The horrid massacre which he continually commits, on the names of people, places, and things,

things, I suppose his translator should share with him.—Both together, they have made vile work of it. In short, it is one of those productions, which you can neither go on to read with patience, or have resolution to lay entirely aside. Many of his political, philosophical, and mercantile reflections and observations, are truly beautiful, and in some places sublime: in others they are so ungenerous, illiberal, and disingenuous, that no catch penny writer of novels hath ever gone beyond him.

His observation, that the English East India Company's servants at Bombay, would one day draw their masters into a precarious and dangerous war with the Mahrattas, hath been verified. Hitherto it hath turned out well: And if the Company's managers at home, have sense enough to force their servants abroad to be quiet with the acquisition of the Island of Salset, which secures at all times provision to Bombay, their mercantile empire on that side of India, may be said to be fixed and permanent. A contrary conduct, will most assuredly shake their possessions all over Asia to their foundations, if not bring ruin on the whole.*

---

*This Letter was written in the end of the year 1776. The writer's opinion of the Mahratta war, so fully expressed, was the same with that of Governor General Hastings; though in obedience to orders from the Company at home, the Governor was obliged to act contrary to it.

THE

The present flourishing state of the Company's affairs in Bengal, where, by your prudence and economy, their debts have been entirely liquidated, and their remittance to Europe, by their annual investments, increased in a sufficient degree to pay their debts there, is an answer to all the Abbe's remarks on tyranny, distress, and mismanagement. I agree with him, that a little more foresight in the country officers of government, might have warded off, in some degree, the dreadful effects of the famine; but that that tremenduous providential visitation, was in the smallest degree increased by the avarice or inhumanity of the Europeans, I deny with great certainty. If ever God made a charitable, just, or good man, the then English Governor of Bengal, John Cartier, Esq. was that man. But at the time we are now speaking of, the government was not sufficiently settled, to have regular returns made of the quantities of rice collected in the different provinces; though the causes of the famine, were plain and alarming enough; and we now are surprised that we did not advert to them. Most certain it is, the general scarcity of grain all the kingdom over, did not strike the imagination of one individual, until it was too late to apply a remedy. The Abbé is quite mistaken, in his account of the seed and harvest time in Bengal. The first crop of rice is planted in May and June, and collected in August and September. However strange it may appear to people at a distance, (the

fact

fact is too well remembered here,) that until the demand for the feed grain, in the month of April, gave the alarm, not a man in the kingdom had the leaſt idea of the dreadful calamity which was on the point to fall upon us. In a few days, rice, which was ſelling at twenty, and twenty two ſeers for a rupee, at the deareſt markets in the kingdom, roſe to eight and ten ſeers. Every body that had money, went to market. The Europeans of all nations, as well as the wealthy country merchants, endeavoured to lay in a ſtock ſufficient to ſerve their ſervants and dependents. The Company did the ſame for their troops, to prevent mutiny. It could not have been otherwiſe in any government in the world. The poor immediately felt the ſevere effects of a rigorous famine. How was it poſſible to prevent it? There was not grain enough left in the kingdom, to ſerve the native inhabitants two months, at one third of their uſual allowance. All that the dictates of charity and humanity could deviſe to be done, was done, by all orders of people, to aſſiſt and relieve the diſtreſſed. It is very poſſible that ſome corn merchants gained fortunes, by having by them a quantity of grain. Was it criminal in them to have had it by them? Is the ſurplus grain in plentiful years, to be thrown into the rivers, to prevent the merchants, who buy it at riſk, and on ſpeculation, from charging a high price for it in years of ſcarcity? What kind of doctrine is this? The truth of the matter is, that

all

all the grain in the kingdom, was consumed by the month of July; and the rigid attachment of the Hindoos to their cast, or religion, is such, that thousands of them lay down and died in the public streets, rather than preserve life at the expence of their cast, by eating what they deem unclean food. As to their dying quietly, rather than plunder the storehouses or granaries of rice, which, as the Abbé says, they saw round them, depend on it there was no such thing. Whilst rice was to be had, they sought it, and it was served out to them with a benevolence and generosity, which did honour to the owners of all denominations. When there was no more left, they preferred death to every other means of preserving life. The sheep, goats, cows, fowls, ducks, geese, and other animals, past by them with impunity. The harmless, inoffensive, innocent Hindoos, died with hunger, in a situation in which no other people on the face of the earth, would have submitted to have gone one day without wholesome food. They bore it tamely, because they knew it was not in the power of their rulers, whom they saw weeping over their misery, with admiration at their fortitude, to relieve them.

The truth once told, where is the use of the pathetic apostrophe, put by the Abbé in the mouths of people, who have had no complaints to make? " *Meer pomp of words, and pedant dissertation.*"

That the famine ought to have been foreseen, I in some degree admit: but that it was foreseen, or any unfair use made of the calamity, when it did come, by Europeans or others, I deny.

In the years 1766 and 1767, rice was so very plenty, that in many places it was not gathered in, as it would not pay the expence of collecting. On this account, less was planted in the year 1768, than had been for many years before. Great quantities of what was planted in 1769, was washed away by the overflowing of the waters; and the extreme and universal drought in 1770, filled our cup of bitters. The scripture account of the Egyptian years of plenty and of scarcity, was literally fulfilled in Bengal. But we are not worthy of having a Prophet, or man of God, sent to warn us of our approaching ruin. It often happens, that the crop suffers from too much, or too little water, in some of the provinces; whilst in other parts, the harvests are as fine and plentiful, as the most sanguine mind can wish; and they supply one another. In no period of time known to record, or to tradition, was there so general a want of rain, as in the year 1770. In vain do men, ignorant of the nature and situation of the kingdom of Bengal, and countries adjacent, talk of relieving it by an import of grain from abroad, in time of scarcity. Had all the tonnage in India, come to Bengal full freight with grain, in the year 1770, it might have relieved

lieved the poor who crowded round the capital, but never could have been of the least use to those dying with want in the provinces. All this the Dutch and French know as well as I do. But the famine was too fair an opportunity to stigmatize their rivals in trade, with being the authors of it, to let such a plausible theme for defamation, slip by unnoticed. Even many of the English, from a diabolical lying spirit of envy, wrote home accounts of the causes of that dreadful calamity, which they must have known to be false. How then could we hope to escape the all-powerful eloquence of the universally knowing Abbé?*

HAVE we not cause to lament the enthusiastic prejudices of our countrymen against their fellow subjects in Bengal, when we find the British Senate

---

* So unexpected was the famine, three months before it happened, at Bengal, that the writer of this Letter, then a capital merchant in Calcutta, had, in the month of April, three ships, of five hundred tons each, called the Lion, the Bahar, and the Cartier, all loading with rice, at the Company's settlement of Ganjam, on the coast of Orissa, which could have been in Bengal River in five days after order should reach them to come home, had their owner conceived the great ruin that was coming on the settlement. He permitted them to proceed to Madrass and Ceylon: And what is more, sold rice at Calcutta, belonging to himself and others, in that very month, at twenty-four seers for the rupee, the like of which was not to be had in July following, four seers for a rupee. In short, if Englishmen have nothing more to answer for, than being, as has been said, the causers of that dreadful calamity, they have nothing to fear in the next world on that account.

entering

entering so far into the belief of the unsupported charges brought against us, as to make a law, prohibiting our buying rice in the provinces? If the farmers have not a ready vend for their grain, as soon as collected, they can neither pay their rent, or plant another crop. The only exporters of grain are the Europeans, in particular the English free merchants settled in Calcutta. They are by this law debarred from buying their grain at the first hand, and of course the quantity exported becomes every year less. How contrary is this to the conduct of the same Legislature in their own country! where they wisely give bounties on the exportation of grain, and thereby secure a good stock in the nation, when ever they please to lay an embargo. But as I shall, in some one of these Letters, prove, beyond the power of controversy, the absurdity of restricting the English settlers in Bengal, from trading in any article the country produces, under proper regulations, I shall say no more of it in this place, but conclude this Letter with putting you in mind, that since the publication of the Abbé's work, it is become indispensibly your duty, to omit no opportunity to collect materials for leaving to your country, and to posterity, an honest, candid, dispassionate, and fair History of Bengal. You were in the service before the capture of Calcutta by the Moors. You have since been employed in every station, from a Resident at the Durbar, to that of Governor General. There is nothing necessary

cessary that you do not know. Your imagination and genius is every way equal to the Abbé's; and you have an advantage which he could not boast, a personal knowledge of every transaction on which it will be necessary for you to treat. I affirm, that you have the knowledge, the abilities, and the honesty, to rescue the actions of your countrymen, from vile allusion, and false aspersion. If you do not do it, may God forgive you. For my part, I shall be very sorry for your indolence, and want of public spirit, if you leave the present, and future generations, in the dark, as to the true history of the transactions of the English in Bengal, from the year 1750, to the 19th day of October, 1774. From that period to the end of your government, terminate when or how it may, the defence of your own honour, calls upon you for another kind of work. And sorry I am to say, that such abilities as yours, must be employed to refute the illiberal and unjust charges, brought against you by a most ignorant, selfish, uncandid, ministerial tool, whose natural and acquired talents, had he been left to shift in the world for himself, could not have lifted him above the rank of a corporal in the guards.— Oh, my country! How will thy honours fade, when an Hastings shall be superseded, or succeeded, by a Clavering, a man the most improper in the world, to be entrusted with so important a charge! Those who wish to see his character drawn very fully, and very justly, have only to look into the

Abbé's

Abbé's works, for the account he gives of the French partizan General Lally, and add to it a most greedy and selfish love of money, and Clavering stands confessed.

WHAT the Abbé says of the oppressions and tyranny, exercised by the English over the French commerce, on the coasts of Malabar and Coromandel, and in Bengal, should be considered as the peevish complaining of a losing gamester. No nation on the face of the earth, would, in a similar situation, have dealt so equitably, and with such moderation, as the English have done, and continue to do, with respect to the French and Dutch traders in India. I most sincerely agree with the Author of the History of the Indies, that *his* countrymen will take the first opportunity of joining the ambitious and discontented Princes, to renew the confusion in Asia; and on that account, I wish to apprise *my* countrymen, that it will be much easier to crush the viper in the shell, than to prevent the effects of his venom, when come to full growth. A stout squadron of ships, built in India, of teke wood, which is by nature calculated to resist for ages, the alternate scorching heats, and vapourous humidity of the climate, will answer the purpose of continuing the power in our hands, much better than by having squadrons sent from Europe. That this may be effected with great ease, and at little expence of men or money to the nation, or to the Company, I pledge myself to make appear. But this Letter is growing long. I therefore must, for the present, take my leave of the Abbé, with many thanks for the pleasure I have had in the perusal of his works. If all his knowledge, and all his philosophy, was insufficient to gloss over his national spleen to my countrymen, he will, I hope, excuse my blunt John Bull like manners, when I affirm, that he has in his history, said many things of the English nation, which are notoriously untrue; and further, that there are many of his assertions, which, as a scholar, a philosopher, and a Christian, he doth not believe himself; but that we owe them entirely to that one single circumstance, of the Abbé's having being born a Frenchman.

LETTER V.

LETTER V.

FROM A

FREE MERCHANT in BENGAL,

TO

WARREN HASTINGS, *Esq.*

HONOURABLE SIR;

IN my First Letter, I pointed out the causes of the decline of the export trade of this kingdom. The effects of those causes are now severely felt: for the Sienda, Surat, and Bombay markets, which formerly were supplied with great quantities of raw silk and sugar from Bengal, have their whole supply of the former article from China, as well as several thousand piculs of the latter, which, with the sugar carried by the Dutch Company's ships to Surat, and English private ships from Batavia to Bombay, hath almost annihilated the sugar trade of Bengal. These evils have taken deep root; for it is now more to the interest of the Company's servants at Bombay, to send a ship loaded with cotton, sandal-wood, and pepper, to China, and load her home with sugar and raw silk, than it is to send her to Bengal; and whilst this continues to be the case, I fear the public spirit of the Company's servants, will not operate sufficiently strong, to induce them to prefer their masters, or even the national interest, to their own. Until within these ten years, very few private ships went from the English settlements in India, to China; and those never brought back raw silk, or powder sugar; for the ships from Bengal could supply the market cheaper. How unluckyly are matters reversed! Nothing is now more common, than for twelve or fifteen English private country ships to be seen in one season at China, loaded with cotton, pepper, sandal-wood, &c. from the Malabar! If bills are to be had at Canton, on any of the European companies, great part of the proceeds of their cargoes, are remitted on account of private persons: the remainder is invested in raw silk, sugar, tea, china ware, &c. and carried back, to the total ruin of the Bengal trade in the two former articles.

It is to be lamented, that the laudable, and even necessary indulgence, granted by the Company to their servants and others, for trading from one part of the East Indies to another, should operate in such a manner, as to cause those very servants to become

become the rivals of their masters. It is the Company's, nay it is the national interest, that their settlements on the coast of Malabar, should, as formerly, be supplied from Bengal, with raw silk and soft sugar. But this never will be the case, whilst those articles are to be had so much cheaper at China than at Bengal. Monopolies and prohibitions, are destructive things; for besides that they check the mercantile spirit in your own national adventurers, they also give a spring to the same spirit in your neighbours and rivals. If the English private gentlemen are forbid this trade under their own colours, they will pursue it under those of other nations. The French, the Portugueze, and the Moors, will supply tonnage to carry on the trade; and the remedy will, in that case, be full as bad, if not worse, than the disease. It will be taking the bread from your own subjects, and casting it to strangers. Accident, which first gave these provinces to the Company, hath also operated in giving this trade a wrong bias. An eagerness to forward private property from Bengal to Europe, by way of China, first gave cause for the China silk and sugar, to rival the Bengal, at the markets of Sienda, Surat, and Bombay. The remittance schemers at Bengal, raised the price of all the articles of export, in the manner set forth in the First Letter. At Bombay, the silk and sugar of Bengal, would not produce their first cost. But the schemers were obliged to go on. They load their ships with

cotton

cotton for China, and there finding no remittance to be had, and raw silk and soft sugar, cheaper than at Bengal, (the ship cannot lie still,) they load back from China to Bombay, with the very articles with which they set out from Bengal; and by this means, in a few years, China robbed Bengal of this whole trade. I have pledged myself to prove my assertions as I go on; but if I was in this place, to introduce the invoices of the ship from Bengal, with silk and sugar, and the account sales at Bombay, and the invoices of the same articles from China, and account sales on the coast of Malabar, it would break the chain of argument, and confuse the whole. Such who doubt my facts, I refer to my book of invoices and account sales, which will follow these letters very shortly.

Bad as our situation is, the remedy is in our own hands. If the sum of 400,000*l.* annually, which, in my First Letter, I proposed to take up at Bengal, for bills on the Company in Europe, is not sufficient to check the wild spirit of remittance in the private cash holders, let it be increased to 600,000*l.* which will put a total stop to so pernicious a project. Keep the cash in the country, and enable the Company to send silk to Bombay, in sufficient quantities to undersell the China silk, and furnish money at Bombay for the use of that presidency, without draining Bengal of its specie, as it has done for many years past.

The

The Company's taking the surplus private money at Bengal, for bills on themselves in Europe, will answer the following good purposes. It will keep the current specie in the kingdom; encourage the silk manufacture, which may be increased to any quantity you please: It will supply the presidency of Bombay with money, and destroy their pernicious trade of importing raw silk from China, to the ports on the Malabar coast, to the ruin of the silk trade in our own provinces; and furnish at Bombay, a capital, with which I propose to connect and extend the Company's European and Asiatic commerce on that side of India.

The Company send from Bengal to Europe, as much raw silk this year, 1777, as will produce about 700,000*l.* sterling.* I do not propose to increase it to more than a million, when I come to treat of the Bengal exports to Europe; and I mention it in this place, only to obviate an objection,

---

*This Letter was written at Bengal in the year 1777. Since the Author has been in England, he has heard much talk about the loss of the Levant Trade. That we do not send so much woollen cloth to Italy, and to Turkey, as formerly, may be true; and the reason is plain. Heretofore, the East India Company imported, *communibus annis*, about 120,000*l.* worth of raw silk from the East Indies; lately, they have imported six times the quantity annually. Does not that account for great part of our (supposed to be lost) Levant Trade, and in a very comfortable way? But croakers never penetrate deeper than the surface. You do not want so much raw silk from Turkey and Italy as formerly, and therefore do not import it.

which

which I forefee will be made to that part of my plan, which leads to an increafe of the export of that article to Bombay; becaufe it will be faid, the fending of raw filk to Bombay, will interfere with the Company's Europe inveftment. So much is the truth on my fide the queftion, that I affirm, on the contrary, that the more filk the Company demand, the eafier will it be to have it made. Mulberry fhrubs to feed, worms to fpin, and men to manufacture filk, will never be wanting in this country, whilft your judicious plan of increafing the inveftment annually, is purfued. Whilft the government are uniformly fteady in their advances, and encouragement, as now, is given to the improvers of the filk manufacture, no quantity which you can pay for, will be wanting. Our evils arifes from a different conduct. Hoarding money up in the treafury, fending fpecie out of the kingdom, fhutting the channel of remittance by the Company's cafh, and curtailing the inveftment, have been the rocks we have fplit on. Whilft you receive the tribute in the manufactured goods of the kingdom, you at once enrich it and your native country; but whilft you ftarve the manufacture to fend cafh abroad, or lock it up, you deftroy the fowl for the golden egg. In the courfe of the laft twenty months, Bombay has been fupplied by Bengal, with thirty-fix lacks of rupees, in money or by bills, at a moft enormous and pernicious difcount. Will any man deny, that it would have been more for

the

the interest of this country, that the Company had sent to Bombay, fifty lacks of rupees in the manufactures of these provinces, though it should have produced no more than the amount sent in cash? Not if he understands the nature of the trade of this kingdom.

WHAT ever it may cost, I maintain it, that the Company should provide annually, to the amount of fifty lacks of rupees in goods, proper for the Gulfs of Mocha, Persia, Bombay, and Surat, the proceeds of which should center in Bombay. Among the invoices will be to be found, the goods properly arranged, which are fit for this purpose. Here I need only mention the names of the several articles; fine and coarse cotton cloths; raw silk, and silk piece goods; sugar, and salt petre; all of which this country is capable of producing the most unlimited quantities. The standard of goodness must never be forgotten; the advances must be made in due time; people secured from oppression; and all chowky duties abolished. With such regulations, the most sanguine imagination is hardly capable of conceiving, to what a degree of opulence this populous and fertile country may be raised.

FROM the fifty lacks of rupees worth of goods sent annually round from Bengal, the proceeds of which should center in Bombay, besides the good

effects

effects mentioned above, others of no less importance will arise. Such a constant and regular supply of the manufactured goods of Bengal, proper for the markets on that side of India, will relieve the Company's servants at Bombay, from the necessity of drawing continually on the government of Bengal, at such amazing discount as is now done; and furnish them with money, not only to supply the deficiency in their current expences, but to assist in preparing goods for the Europe and China market; and by that means, send stock to enable the Company to answer the bills which must inevitably, for some years, be drawn on them from Bengal, to turn the current of private remittance into our own channel.

It very often happens, that the presidency at Bombay have not stock sufficient, or even credit, to raise money to compleat the investment indented for by the Company. The consequence of this is, that one, and sometimes two of their ships, which the Company expect will return with pepper, Surat and Cambaya piece goods, &c. are obliged to be sent round to the other presidencies in quest of cargoes.—Who doth not see that such injudicious management would ruin individuals? The Company, from its credit and permanency, is enabled to stand the shock.—But how are the Directors to be defended? Why truly by their indolence or ignorance; for they never hitherto, have thought of connecting,

connecting, or combining, the trade in India with the trade in Europe, in such a manner, as that they should mutually support each other, they know that. If no cargo is ready at one presidency, the managers there will send the ship to another, and that gives the opportunity of serving a favourite Captain: otherwise what is meant by their continual recommendation, of sending such or such a ship a country voyage, when they must, or ought to know, they have properly speaking, no country trade carried on for the Company, from port to port in India?

With the cargoes of the ships outward bound to Bombay, with the proceeds of the Company's revenue on the Island, the custom-house collections, and the supply from Bengal, a great fund will be established at that presidency, to carry on the mercantile concerns of the Company. I say their mercantile concerns, because I would wish to have them suppress the military spirit for conquest and dominion, and come back to their first mercantile principles. How foreign is it to the spirit which the constitution should naturally inspire, to see their servants at Bombay, at one and the same time, enlarging their military establishment, and reducing that of the marine! If they are not positively tied down, never to extend their conquests beyond the Island of Salset, in vain will you establish a fund for trade. Bring the younger servants back to their

offices,

offices, and oblige them to study the interests of their employers, on the constitutional principles of the Company's charter, in the whole of which, the words conquest and dominion are not to be found, or no national good can arise from your possessions on that side India. If the Proprietors of India Stock, will be at the pains to examine the annual military, civil, and marine expences, at Bombay, and add to those the freight paid for ships, taken up for that part of the service, and the sum total of the invoices of goods sent out from Europe on those ships, and then observe, that all the returns which are made to defray such enormous expences, is a cargo or two of pepper, one of piece goods, and every second year a cargo of coffee, they would soon be convinced, that were their dividends to arise out of such pitiful returns, how soon they would sink to nothing. It is the rich mine in Bengal, which has hitherto supported such unjustifiable, injudicious, and accumulated expences: But that is not inexhaustible. If a war with France breaks out, from whence are the funds to arise to support such consuming establishments? The answer is easy enough; the military men shall give it.—Let us go, say they, into the Mahratta country, and we will conquer for you provinces in abundance, the territorial revenue of which shall answer all your demands.—I am quite sick of hearing such doctrine. We have conquered more than once, until we have been on the brink of ruin. For God's sake let us draw

draw some benefit from dear bought experience, and not, by grasping at what can never be of the least use to us as a mercantile people, lose the advantages we may, and ought to draw, from our present situation as such.*

The Company have, at no period of time, had stock in hand sufficient at Bombay, to furnish one years investment in advance, which has been a great disadvantage to their affairs; for by not knowing what goods were, or could, with the annual stock in hand, be provided, they took their annual ships up at a venture, rather than on a fixed plan. If one entire cargo of the usual sorts of piece goods, half a one of coffee, and three entire cargoes of pepper, were always ready in their warehouses at Bombay, and on the Malabar coast, exclusive of what was indented for the service of the current year, they could at all times command goods for the markets in Europe, and be sure of the return of the ships in regular rotation, and not have them at a most ruinous expence of demurrage, running about India to seek for cargoes. This appears to me to be the first step which ought to be taken on

---

* It is not vanity which induces the Author to note that these Letters were written in 1776 and 1777; it is the desire he has of doing justice to the man to whom they are addressed. Mr. Hastings dreaded, and would, if he could, have prevented the pernicious Mahratta war, which has since produced the distresses the Author foretold.

the coast of Malabar; and that the government there should, in the month of January every year, transmit to Bengal, a concise statement of their stock of cash, and saleable goods on hand, what would be their probable expences for the current year, and a list of such Bengal goods, as would be most proper to send them to make good the deficiency. This list would be at Bengal in time to go home with the April packet, and the Governor General and Councils answer to it; by which the Company would know what dependence they could place on the government of Bengal, for their necessary annual returns from Bombay. As things are managed at present, they are at no kind of certainty whatever; and this is one of the causes why they sometimes send out five ships to the Malabar coast, and have but three, two, and sometimes one, return loaded from that side of India. The others are sent about from presidency to presidency, at an enormous expence to the Company, in quest of a returning cargo, and carrying goods for the benefit of the Captain only.

With such a stock in hand as is mentioned above, the Directors would act with some degree of certainty. If the Europe markets required an additional quantity of piece goods, coffee, pepper, &c. the Company would have but to order it, and it would come home on the returning ships.

That

THAT all the Company's merchant ships outward bound, ought to be clear of the Channel by the first of April, to insure them a tolerable passage to India, is well known to many in the direction. Why they are detained later, no good reason can be given. The old plea of keeping a ship or two, until the election was over, to let their friends abroad know who was to govern for the year, is now over. The state have reduced the annual supply of new Directors, to the small number of six. Now if the whole of the East India Proprietors of Stock, are so well broken in and bitted, as to admit of the Minister sending a card with the names of six servile dependents of his own, to fill up the annual vacancies, I own I know not what to say. But if, as I hope, there is yet left virtue sufficient among the independent Proprietors of Stock, to judge for themselves, I do not imagine that the nation in general is so depraved, but that six men may be annually found, who possess the necessary qualifications of honour, integrity, knowledge, and abilities, to conduct this great branch of the national commerce, on the true mercantile principles: men who, from being inspired with true patriotism, will have the national honour, and Company's interest, ever in view; who will suffer no paltry inclination to serve individuals, to be an inducement to sacrifice their public trust. London surely is not yet become such a sink of iniquity, such a Sodom and Gomorrah, but that six rich
merchants

merchants are to be found, in whose hands this branch of the national mercantile honour, may be placed with safety.

PLACE me twenty-four such men as described above, in the direction, the second Wednesday in April, and by the first of July, they will have ready, to send from London by the July packet, a list of the ships they propose to send to each of their settlements in India the coming season, with an account of what goods they will carry out, and what returns they expect by them. These papers will be circulated to all their principal, as well as subordinate settlements, as soon as they arrive, and each factory will know what goods they are to have to sell, and what returns they are expected to prepare. They will make their ability, or inability, known to the presidency on which they are dependent, and assistance will be given in time, to enable them to comply with the Company's orders.

WILL it not surprise any man to know, that the Company carry on their mercantile correspondence with their four presidencies, in as secret and mysterious a manner, as if they were enemies to one another; and by such ridiculous conduct, have, in many instances, made them so. The presidency at Bengal, know no more what orders, or what goods, are sent from Europe to Bombay, than if they were a colony of Russians. No statements are ever sent from

from presidency to presidency, as they are not amenable but to the Company. They correspond on the terms of independent states. The government of Bombay and Bencoolen, draw bills on Bengal, because they want money, but assign no reason for their drawing; and this facility of obtaining cash, has been the cause of a great profusion of expence at the former of those presidencies. The managers at home, not feeling the inconveniency of furnishing the money, examine so little into it, that I fancy it would be difficult to find, in all the Company's correspondence with Bombay, one single paragraph, tending to check such a wanton waste of property. It is now grown into such a habit, that the Bombay gentlemen will not have the least patience to wait the supplies, but have, within the course of twelve months, sent down three different vessels to Bengal for money; and our simpletons here have opened their veins, and let them suck their hearts blood; for the sending the current specie of a mercantile country away, which hath no present hopes of a speedy supply, is literally such. If it can be proved, and I shrewdly suspect that it may, that for five years past, the presidency of Bombay, have had from Bengal, more money, in cash and bills, than the whole amount of the invoices of the goods they have transmitted, within the same period of time, to the Company in Europe, tell me, ye wise men, how long this will last? Can such enormous profusion be supported?

And what will be your situation, in case of a war with France?

So little connected, and so unameanable, are these injudicious servants of an ill managed Company, to one another, that it is notoriously known, that the gentlemen at Bombay, have supplied the freebooter Hyder Ally, with arms and amunition on the coast of Malabar, when he was preparing to, and actually on his march, to attack the Carnatic. Can any human policy be more ridiculous, than that the Bombay presidency, should write to the Company in the most pressing manner, for leave to take advantage of the confusions in the Mahratta government, by joining one party, in order to extort some concessions from them; whilst the presidency at Bengal, at a great expence, was sending over land to the Mahratta court, at Delhi, a Lieutenant-Colonel as an Ambassador, to make a peace with them. At Madrass, the senior civil servants, inspired by the military, confine their Governor, and usurp the government. The Governor General and Council of Bengal, approve the measure, and promise to support the new administration. The Governor and Council at Bombay, declare they will not know them, but address to Lord Pigot. Is not this, in the scripture language, a house divided against itself? Tell me, ye military merchants, how long will it stand?

The ruin which I plainly foresee, the military spirit will bring on this beneficial branch of the trade of my country, is continually staring me in the face, and carrying me away from my argument. It is grown to such a height, that it almost requires a providential interposition to save us. Surely the independent Proprietors will step in, and examine minutely the conduct of the Directors, and not permit a venal and ignorant majority, longer to squander away their property, and the national honour. Let the man, or, if it were more, the men, who, by their interest and influence, sent out Sir Robert Fletcher twice, to the command of the army on the coast, after he had been broke by a court martial, for fomenting the discontent of the army, at the resignation in Bengal, and repeatedly gave him the opportunity to disturb the government of Mr. Dupree, and to imprison Lord Pigot; let them, I say, reflect on the consequences of supporting such military firebrands, in opposition to the real mercantile interest of the East India Company, whose commercial prosperity is become so necessary to the honour and natural interest of their country.—But to return———

My twenty-four Directors having determined on the number of ships which will be necessary to carry out the million and a half of goods of the mother country, and bring home the cargoes from Asia, which I have engaged shall produce three times that sum in Europe, they will not be at a loss how to dispose of them. They will go loaded out, and come loaded home, for the Company, and not for the masters. No canvassing for particular voyages, will disturb their councils. They will be men of honour, pleased and happy, with the credit of being trusted with the care of public property. But as they are but men, and liable to the weakness and foibles of men, they will, by good regulations, calculated for the interest of the Company, and dispatch of business, put it out even of their own power, to act improperly. The ships to be first taken up, are known from the date of their arrival at the Island of St. Helena, homeward bound the last voyage. The number wanted for all the presidencies once fixed, let so many tickets, with the name of the presidency on them, as answer the number of the ships, be put into an urn, and the names of the freighted ships in another, and let the drawing determine the voyage. The four or five tickets with the name of Bombay on them, should determine that to be the voyage of the ships, the names of which were drawn at the same time; and so of the rest. It might not be thought an improper place, to introduce here, my plan for regulating the private trade, to be allowed to the Captain and Officers of each ship; but as it will branch out into so many divisions and subdivisions, and will include indulgences to all orders of the Company's servants abroad, it will require a Letter of itself,

if

if I find time, and have courage to attempt it. I must own I begin to be a little afraid of touching on it at all; as to give the real reasons for abolishing the present mode of conducting the private trade, and substituting another in its room, will lead me into such a detail of the artful, low, un-gentleman-like evasions, practised in the service, as would make it dangerous for me to engage in. Such tampering with tradesmen, to set their names to false bills of parcels; such bribing the Company's officers on the ships going out, and the King's and Company's officers, on their coming home; such smuggling, false swearing, paltry cunning, and contemptible lying, as would most likely deter many honest parents, from breeding their children up in a service, where the infamous practices they are witness to, the very first voyage, root out for ever from their young minds, every idea of virtue and morality. If I do attempt to sketch a plan for conducting the private trade in the service, I most assuredly will do it with the same freedom as I treat of the public commerce; and I wish the present Captains, and present Officers, not to suppose themselves the men intended, when I describe a practice, which, in its operations, is destructive to our national character, for mercantile probity, and common honesty. I will mention no names of swearing Captains, or forswearing Officers; perjured, or forging Pursers. Let them not lay to my charge, the internal twitchings of that never dying monitor, their own conscience; that when I say a thing is frequently done, gives hints that I mean them, because they did it. Let them cease to be perjured knaves, and the satire falls to the ground. After all, as I believe the fault to be originally in the managers, who, from false notions of economy, and glove-like consciences, make roguery necessary to a subsistence in the service, if, in my investigation, I chance to probe the evil to the bottom, and in so doing, give pain to the diseased, I do at the same time promise them, a mild, equitable, and easy remedy.

Bombay is most certainly the place best calculated in all India, at which to form a naval power. The magazines of naval stores, both for the King and Company's use, must be laid up there. The noble docks it now has, and more, which in time it may have, makes it a place of the utmost importance to the Company, and to the nation. I want to make it the great emporium of trade for the western side of India—Not a mere Gibraltar; a barrack for troops, or magazine for military stores. The harbour is safe and capacious. Your fleet will give protection to the merchants who may frequent it from Persia, Arabia, Abyssinia, the Red Sea, and Africa; as well as from the coast of Gandell, Sienda, Guzurat, Cambaya, and the whole of the Mahratta dominions on the Malabar. I will not say that it should at once be made a free port, because

cause at present we are poor; but I most sincerely wish it may soon become so; and in the interim, would have no kind of duties levied on the goods, sent from Bengal for sale on that side of India. It would astonish any man, to know what a concourse of vessels would flock from all the above mentioned dominions to Bombay, when they were once assured of your passes of protection, (for what power would dare to insult your flag?) and come with a certainty of finding the Bengal goods, proper for their different countries, wrought up to their primitive goodness, and on reasonable terms. Every thing you want for the Company in Europe, or at China, would be brought home to your own doors; and golden showers of money to make good the balance, which would be for ever in your favour. No people who have ever yet traded by sea to India, have had it so much in their power to make permanent a mercantile empire, as the English, since their acquisition of Bengal. Great as our mistakes have been, we have yet time to look back to first principles. You, Sir, are setting the example in Bengal. May the influence of your conduct extend to the Malabar, and save us from that prelude to a general ruin of our Asiatic commerce, a continental war with the Mahrattas.

It seems that the Court of Directors, by taking up four or five ships annually for Bombay, when at most they can have cargoes ready but for three,

including

including the coffee ship, would perſuade the public, that it is neceſſary to be at the expence of one or two additional ſhips, to carry out men and ſtores for their army and marine at that preſidency. If this really be the caſe, why not take an advantage for the Company, which is conſtantly ſolicited, and has been very often granted to, individuals? A ſhip which has run out her four voyages in the Company's ſervice, is not ſo decayed as to be unfit to go a fifth. The reaſon which prevents her being taken up a fifth time, is, that the freight the Company pay is ſo ample, that they can always have new ſhips at the ſame rate as an old one, and on that account, it is a good rule that a ſhip ſhall make but four voyages in their ſervice. But it is by no means an economical one, that ſhe ſhall be always ten, often twelve, and ſometimes fifteen years, in executing what may be performed ſometimes in ſeven, and always in eight years. But rigid economy is by no means the characteriſtic of the managers for the Eaſt India Company. They enter into the direction with a declared intention to ſerve their private friends, and in general keep ſo cloſe to that their avowed principle of action, that they very ſeldom think of the Company.

THE very beſt of the ſhips which have ſerved out their time, is to be bought for 1500*l*. For 6000*l*. more they may be fitted out and victualled for the run to Bombay, ſo as to ſubſiſt during the voyage,

one

hundred recruits for their army, and one hundred seamen for the marine; and the ship, on her arrival in India, will sell, with her stores, for her first cost and outfit, that is 7500*l*. and the Company would have transported to their settlements, at no kind of expence, three hundred tons of stores, and two hundred recruits for her army and marine. Compare this with their practice of a Bombay and and China, and a Bombay and Bengal ship, where every sacrifice is made to favour the commander, to the ruin of the Company, and scandal of their Directors.

The fact as above related, is so notoriously true, that I run a greater risk of being laughed at for publishing what every body knows, than to have the matter controverted. Is it not then very extraordinary, that so plain, equitable, and easy a method, is not pursued, when it would most assuredly save to the Company, 25,000*l*. every year? But it would leave two ships untaken up, and prevent two favourite Captains from making their fortunes. I have known one of those important men (I mean a Captain of one of the Company's ships) sent from Bombay with six hundred bales of cotton to Bengal, in the month of September, with orders to return to Bombay in the following March, act so lubberly in the passage, as not to arrive in Bengal River till the end of February, and whilst there, entering a protest against the Governor and Council, for not

dispatching

dispatching of him in time to return from Bombay to Europe the same season; though this was, from his late arrival, become utterly impossible: yet the protest served the purpose of throwing the whole weight of the expence on the Company, and saved the owners on her return to Europe. This is one instance, selected from many hundreds, where a ship has been sent out of her way, at an improper season of the year, for no other reason in the world, but to serve the Captain. The freight of the six hundred bales of cotton down to the Bay, and of three thousand bags of salt p tre back, comes to 2625*l.* the demurrage of the ship for one whole year, at twenty pounds per diem, comes to 7300*l.* to this must be added the disappointment and expence the Company were unnecessarily put to, if goods were ready with which to have sent the ship home from Bombay in March, or the folly (to say no worse) of taking the ship up at all, if there was no returning cargo ready for her. I know the Directors, the Owners, and the Commanders, have been so blended and knit together, that I have not the least doubt, but that some half starved, shoeless, threadbare, garretteer grammarian, will be employed to deny the facts, abuse the author, and criticise on the language of these truth speaking papers, and his pay will be carried to the head of secret service charges. If the Proprietors will be so duped, as not to examine into the merits of their own cause, let them sleep on. I have a national purpose in
view

view in writing thefe Letters. The proper management of the trade to Afia, is of the higheft importance to the profperity of Great Britain It muft be conducted by an intermediate body between the ftate and individuals, conftituted fomething like the prefent Company. But their managers fhould be public fpirited, and honeft men; and in order to their being fo, I take now and then an opportunity to obferve, that it is well known, that their predeceffors were confummate rogues, and by their ill management, brought difhonour on their country.

During the late war, great complaints were made in England, of the want of large timber for the ufe of the royal navy. It has fince gone fo far, as to raife a jealoufy of the Eaft India Company, for building fuch large fhips for their fervice, as are the Befborough, Morfe, Grafton, &c. To go about to affign the real reafon, which gave caufe to the owners to build fuch unweildy fhips, to ferve as mere merchant-men, would lead me again into that kind of inveftigation, which I have but this moment quitted; and which, however neceffary to be ufed now and then *in terrorem*, doth by no means lead to the point I have in view, which is a better management in future, not retrofpection into what is paft; nor fhall I ufe it but in fupport of my affertions, that the Eaft India Company's managers at home, have made a perpetual facrifice of their
intereft

interest for the advantage of individuals, and connived at a military spirit in their servants abroad, which leads to the utter ruin of the national trade to Asia.

Had the ships above mentioned, and others of the same dimensions, been pierced to carry fifty guns, as the French have ever done their East India ships, then indeed they might have been armed in time of war, in such a manner, as to have served as convoy to the other ships of the Company, or occasionally been brought into the line; but to build them half as large again as the Company's other ships, and charter them for the same tonnage, was a scandalous waste of the national stock of timber; and for reasons so iniquitous, that I shall not mention them.

It is in time of peace, that all wise nations prepare for war. There is not a doubt, but that our possessions in Asia must be protected by our naval power. It is clear that government think so. For on the least alarm of the French sending a force to the Isles of France, a squadron is immediately dispatched by the court of London, to the coast of Malabar or Coromandel. This, whether the alarm be true or false, is unavoidably attended with a great expence of ships, men, and money. The nation can bear the latter much better than the two former; and this reflection leads me back to the
consideration

consideration of the first link of my great combining chain, which I propose to extend round every branch of the national trade to the East Indies, and by so doing, point out the way to give life, spirit, strength, and permanency to the whole, and thereby render it invulnerable to the busy, active, artful, and designing views of our jealous rivals, and natural enemies, the French.

THE Company send five ships annually to Bombay. Their servants there, for want of money, find it difficult to return them three. To remove this difficulty, I am for taking money at Bengal, with which to provide proper goods to be sent to Bombay, and give bills on the Company for what the Bengal presidency cannot spare.—But how, say the Directors, are we to have it sent us home? We want no more pepper, coffee, Surat, Cambaya, or other piece goods, from that side of India.—If that is really the case, Gentlemen, are you not ashamed to keep up, at such an astonishing expence, fleets, armies, and factories, on that side the peninsula, to furnish three ships cargoes only? You have done with conquests; for if that is permitted you one inch further than what you now possess, reasons, such as you and your military servants can produce, will not be wanting to carry the British flag to Delhi, to Agra, to Ava, to Tartary, and Peking in China. You must be tied down to Salset; the fallacious ideas of accumulating territorial

revenue

revenue put our of your heads, or you out of your posts; and your agents abroad be set down to sorting of cloth, and sifting the dust out of pepper. When you are thus brought back to your reason, and to the occupation long and successfully practised by your predecessors of old time, on the principles of the charter, you will not want vend for double the quantity annually; nor we, here, the means of sending it to you. But you are not the people with whom I wish to argue. I address the great mercantile Governor Hastings, and appeal to the common sense of the nation. It is your mal-administration, your ignorance, your selfishness, and other iniquity, that continually occurs, and lead me out of my argument into these wild digressions.

If more Malabar pepper than what you now send home, cannot be vended in Europe to good advantage, (which I am so stubborn as not to believe,) you never can overstock the markets at China; and as your trade to China is a trade of necessity, and must be carried on, I wish to have it done at as little expence of money to the nation as possible. I shall therefore, in all my arguments, consider our trade with China rather as a channel, by which the near proceeds of the national estate in Asia, may be remitted to the least disadvantage, than as a traffic of choice. If you order home a greater quantity of pepper, and other goods, from the

the Malabar, so much the better; the remittance is eligible, because it is more direct; the freight and other charges, less; and you consequently, better able to undersell your European rivals: However, you may determine that point. Your servants there must have in charge, to provide cotton and pepper for the China market, in sufficient quantities to load annually three or four ships. The means by which I propose to pay for, and convey it to China, will appear in its proper place.

EXPERIENCE hath long since shewn, that ships built with oak, and joined together with wooden trunnels, are by no means so well calculated to resist the extremes of heat and damp, in the tropical latitudes of Asia, as the ships which are built in India of tekewood, and bound with iron spikes and bolts. There is vast plenty of tekewood in Asia, particularly on the Malabar coast, both to the north and south of Bombay. It is well known to Sir George Pococke, and many other great sea officers, that the Company have there a well furnished marine yard, with three very large and good dry docks, and slips for building ships of sufficient burthen for the Company's service as merchantmen. I will say nothing on the utility, or inutility, of the state permitting the Company to build ships there, on which to transport their Asiatic merchandize to Europe, because I am not a competent judge of the matter, as it relates to the necessity of

using

using none but ships built in the mother country, for the purpose of national trade, as set forth in that great palladium of English commerce, the act of navigation. But I could wish to have a law passed, by which the Company should be permitted to build two ships annually, at Bombay, of teke-wood, in every respect like unto the best constructed ships in the royal navy, carrying each sixty guns. With such a grant, a very powerful naval force might be gradually, and almost imperceptibly, formed of ships, every way better calculated to resist the inclemency of the climate, and ready to arm, when ever the exigencies of the state shall require them to be armed. As to finding employment for them in times of peace, or manning of them in times of war, there will be no difficulty in effecting either, provided the government will consent, that when ever they shall find it for the good of the state, to order any of these ships into commission, the Captains then in command of them, shall take the rank that day as post Captains, and the Officers receive commissions as Lieutenants in the royal navy, provided there be no legal objections to their becoming King's Officers, and that they themselves are willing to serve. Besides this, the government must pay to the Company, the first cost and outfit of the ship and her stores.

The number of men necessary to navigate these ships as merchant-men, I suppose to be about one hundred

hundred and sixty seamen, exclusive of officers: these, together with their guns, cordage, sailcloth, and sundry other stores, not to be had in India, must be sent out annually on the store ships above mentioned; and as those store ships are to be sold in India, it will by no means be difficult to procure good commanders and active officers, when they know, that on their arrival at Bombay, they will be removed into line of battle ships, which, in case of necessity, will be taken into the King's service, and so have an honourable provision for life. For the first year after the ships are built, I would have them employed on the Malabar coast as guard ships, with one tier of their guns mounted; in which time, the men would learn their exercise; the good qualities or defects of the ships, would be discovered; and the marine force at Bombay, be properly augmented with a respectable addition, always ready to support the Company's interest, and render service to their country, when called out to action. Who does not see, that with two such ships continually on the coast, that an immediate reduction may be made both on the Company's land and sea forces, fully adequate to the expence of manning and victualling of them? If the ships should be called to augment the King's squadron, before an opportunity offers to man them complete, there will always be to be found at such a populous trading town, and free mercantile port, as I hope Bombay will shortly be, Lascars, Coffrees,

frees, and other Afiatic feamen, in plenty, to complete the neceffary number. Moft of the land forces may ferve as marines, if action is expected; for I know of no other ufe they will be of; for I hope we have done with continental wars; and that man knows little of the Afiatics, who conceives that they will come to attack you on your Iflands. As for the French, arm yourfelves as Englifhmen ought ever to be armed, and let them attempt it if they dare.

LEAST any naval officer fhould fneer at my plan for manning fhips occafionally for the King's fervice, I wifh to remind him of the three fea engagements, which happened in India during the laft war, in which thofe great naval officers, Sir George Pococke and Admiral Stevens, commanded. We kept the fea, it is true, and the French left it, but not till they had effected what they came to effect, throwing fupplies into their garrifons on fhore. They each time bore up to, or lay by for the Britifh fquadron. One fhip of the French, was run on fhore in the firft action. In all the three we gained honour, it muft be admitted; but it coft us many lives, and difabled many of our fhips, particularly in the fecond engagement. Yet in no one of thofe furious actions, was there more than four, or at moft five, of the French King's line of battle fhips prefent; all the others were the French Company's trading fhips, more than half manned with Coffrees.

If

If ever a people were drubbed who won the battle, the English squadron, under the command of Sir George Pococke, in the East Indies, had that honour on the 3d day of August, in the year of our Lord 1758. Will a French Officer dare attempt against an English squadron, what an English Officer, in similar circumstances, would not attempt against a French one? I will not believe it. I have known many naval officers on service in the East Indies, but never was acquainted with one of them, who, had he had the honour to have commanded one of the King of England's sixty gun ships, manned with two hundred English seamen, and three hundred Lascars, Coffrees, and other natives of Asia, that would have declined coming to action with the best French ship of war that ever appeared in those seas. I am not an advocate for using foreigners to man the royal navy; but if Englishmen are not to be had in those distant regions, to full man the ships in time of war, the alternative is not a bad one. Nor will any English Admiral hesitate to strengthen his squadron with the Company's ships of war, constructed, armed, and manned, as above mentioned.*

---

* The Author has, since the writing of this Letter, been employed to man and command two forty-four gun ships, to reinforce the King's squadron under Sir Edward Vernon, and that officer expressed great pleasure at receiving such assistance, though the ships were manned half and half, as above mentioned.

As I propose to have two of those ships built every year at Bombay, in times of peace, and more than that number will not be wanting to guard the Malabar, the two firſt built ships muſt prepare to quit the coaſt, as ſoon as the others are ready to ſupply their places. In time of peace, the Company will neither want, nor can well afford, to keep above two ſhips of ſuch force in commiſſion. It muſt, therefore, be ſo managed, that at the time they are relieved, that very rich and full cargoes of Malabar goods, be provided for them; viz. cotton, pepper, ſandal-wood, ſhark fins, &c. with which to go to China, and from thence load home to Europe. In the courſe of a few years, a very formidable ſquadron would be collected, built of the beſt wood in the world, to reſiſt the heats and damps of the Indian climate. They will ſuit the Company's trade for any part of India, except Bengal; and if kept in conſtant employment, do much more ſervice for leſs money, than is paid now for the freight ſhips. The additional men which they would require in time of war, would not amount to ſo much as the difference of freight paid for the ſhips of individuals. They would ſerve as convoy for the Company's other ſhips, both out and home; would be at all times ready to augment the King's ſquadrons, if wanted; and would make eight voyages from and to India, inſtead of four, in leſs time, and at much leſs expence. I will, in the courſe of theſe Letters, give a ſketch

of

of what one of these ships would cost the Company, and what services she would render in the course of ten years, and what such service would cost them on their present plan.

The Company should go on to build, until they had eight of those ships to leave India every year; that is about one third of their number of ships expected home; four of these should be from China, and two from Bombay; the St. Helena and Bencoolen storeship, and the Madrass October ship. In time of war, their homeward bound ships should rendezvous at St. Helena; and all those which arrived by the first of March, should sail as the first division, under convoy of three of the sixty gun ships; the second division on or before the fifteenth of May, with three more of the armed ships; and the other two stay to collect the remainder of the ships of the season, and sail in one or two divisions, as might appear best for the interest of the Company. The China ships should pass the Straits of Sunda, or Malacca, in two divisions, having with them two of the armed ships. And this arrangement would give such security to their trade, that nothing could injure it, without distressing the government for ships for convoy, which they sometimes can but ill spare; and very often so late, that the homeward bound ships are obliged to sail from St. Helena without them.

For

For my own part, I own myself to be so sanguine in my expectations, that Bengal will be able to supply in a very few years, under your management, the means of sending three or four of these ships, from the Malabar coast to China, richly laden with proper cargoes, to furnish tea, raw silk, and china ware, for their returning cargoes to Europe, that I have not a doubt about it. All I ask, is honest men for our managers, good allowance for Captains and Officers, and rigid discipline to keep them to their duty.

Having laid the foundation for a future addition of marine force for the use of my country, I would proceed to the further connecting of our Asiatic commerce, but am called aside by that most extraordinary genius, the Author of the History of the East and West Indies.

There is such animating descriptions of people, places, and things, in every part of the Abbé's works, that except in the accounts of transactions at which a man has himself been present, one can hardly withhold an implicit belief of every thing he says. Had I not had an intimate knowledge of the transactions that have happened on the continent of India, in which the European nations have been concerned, for these twenty-five years past, and been myself, more than once, trading at every port, from Surat along the coasts of Malabar and
Cromandel

Coromandel to Bengal, as well as in the Gulfs of Mocha and Persia, I should not have doubted the Abbé's description of them, any more than I did his account of any other nation, place, or people, whom I have never seen or heard of. But when I find him stating facts falsely, and then arguing on them, and drawing conclusions as if they were true, I own it raises in my mind, a kind of involuntary scepticism to all historical anecdotes, except they come much better authenticated than many of the Abbé's, which relate to affairs and transactions in India.

I HAVE heard that Mr. Robertson, the writer of the Life of the Emperor Charles V. had some thoughts of writing the History of the East Indies, but dropped it on the Abbé's History coming out. I am sorry for this; because a work of that kind, impartially drawn up, would be universally useful. There are I am certain, authentic documents sufficient in Europe, to ascertain every important fact which need to be known. Nor would so respectable an historian be refused access to them in Portugal, France, Holland, or England. Shakespeare's historical plays, which treat of the wars between the Houses of York and Lancaster, contain a better History of England, during the reigns of the Princes of those Houses, than the Abbé's doth of the transactions which have passed in India since the year 1740.

The Abbé, in the second volume and fifth book of his history, as translated by Justamond, determines, that it is for the interest of Europe in general, and each maritime state in particular, that a brisk trade should be carried on with that part of Asia called India; that it is the cause of population in a much greater proportion, than it causes the destruction of the human species; and instances the populousness of the maritime states in proof of his assertions. He also proves, that by imitating the commodities of Asia, industry hath been greatly increased in Europe; and that no part of its products enervates or weakens, the constitutions of the Europeans, when consumed in Europe. That the trade to Asia increases the consumption of the produce of Europe, and multiplies our employments. That finding a vend for a part of the wealth of Mexico and Peru, it causes the mines of those kingdoms to be wrought with greater spirit; and that European nations, being the carriers of the east and western worlds, benefit extremely from the discovery of, and trade to both: And concludes, and I think very justly, that since the communication Europe hath kept up with Asia and America, its inhabitants are become more numerous, more civilized, more humane, and infinitely richer. In the same volume and book, page the 3d, the Abbé seems to lament that the French were tedious and slow, and a long time before they availed themselves of their power in India, to attempt

tempt the subversion of the Mogul empire. When they did attempt it, they succeeded so far as to ruin for a time, those noble provinces, and destroy entirely their own beneficial trade to India, as the Portugueze had done before them; and in which pernicious scheme, I much fear, the English will be too apt to follow their example. It is this epidemical infatuation for conquest of which I complain It is big with the destruction of the British commerce to Asia; and which to prevent, I would with pleasure lay down my life, if that would impede its progress. Had I the great abilities of the Abbé, I would paint the mistakes of my countrymen in such lively colours, that should draw their attention over to their real and true interests; and warn them in time of the ruin, into which they seem to be so blindly precipitating themselves and their country.

I MUST quote entire, the next paragraph in the same page of the Abbé's works, because I never saw such great truths, and such gross mistakes, blended together in so few words.

'THE English, more prudent, did not attempt
'to aggrandize themselves, until they had stripped
'the French of their acquisitions, and till no rival
'nation could contend with them. The certainty
'of having none but the natives to contend with,
'determined them to fall on Bengal. It was the
'province

'province of all India, which afforded most com-
'modities fit for the markets of Asia and Europe,
'and was likely to consume most of their manu-
'factures, and also that which their flag could best
'protect, having the advantage of great rivers they
'have conquered; and they flatter themselves,
'they shall long enjoy the fruit of their victory.'

It is notorious, even from the Abbé's own History, that the English never stirred out of their factories, on the Coromandel coast, until they saw that the success which the French met with in the war which terminated in 1748, had turned their heads to conquest and dominion. The loss of Madrass, and the unsuccessful attempt made by Boscawen on Pondicherry, had weakened the English extremely in the Carnatic. The French thought the opportunity fair to drive them off the coast entirely; and very possibly they would have succeeded, but for the efforts of the brave Lawrence, and his intrepid scholar in the art of war, Clive. The troops of both nations acted as auxiliaries to Princes of the country; and it must be admitted, that both sides took every opportunity to strengthen their interest all over the Deccan; but neither the French or the English, had the most distant idea of attempting a conquest of Bengal. When the troubles commenced in 1756, the French had at Chandernagore, and their settlements in that kingdom, three times the force that the English had at Calcutta,

cutta, and their out factories: It is true that at this period, a war was expected to break out between the two nations in Europe, on account of their American disputes: But no idea was formed, or could be formed, of a conquest of Bengal, when the injudicious conduct of Drake, the Governor of Calcutta, involved the whole settlement in ruin, and brought on the expulsion of his countrymen. This was one of those accidents, which unexpectedly lead the way to most extraordinary events. The English happened to have in India, and unemployed, four ships of the line, commanded by some of the best officers the nation could ever boast. A Watson carried the flag, and a Speke commanded the flag ship, which was to lead the way over those dangerous sands the Brasses, which seem to forbid the entrance of large ships into the River of Bengal. But nature herself is sometimes obliged to give way to true heroism. Even one Smith, a pilot, had the glorious flame lighted up in his mind. Inspired by the intrepid spirit of Speke, he was induced to undertake what, unsupported by such a hero, his cooler reason would have deterred him from attempting. The ships were carried safely into the river; and the greatest of all English soldiers (Clive) landed with a handful of men. He dispersed the millions who opposed him; and the English flag was again seen to fly in their own little territory. Even yet no conquest of the country was thought of. It would lead me too far out of my way, to

say

say what made it neceſſary at length to ſubdue it: We have it, and, as the Abbé ſays, flatter ourſelves we ſhall keep it; nor is ſuch flattery ill founded, if my countrymen are not chained down by inevitable fate, to work out their own undoing. Save them, moſt gracious God; I beſeech thee, ſave them. Bury in the overflowings of thy infinite mercy, their errors and miſtakes. Continue you to us the diſintereſted, the generous, the manly, and charitable *Haſtings*; and recall the avenging demon, parent of informers, and father of lies, *Clavering*.

The Abbé declares, that the Engliſh having ſtripped the French of their acquiſitions, and having no European nation to contend with, determined them to fall on Bengal. There never was an aſſertion ſo void of truth. At the breaking out of the war in 1756, the French were ſuperior in power to the Engliſh, in every part of India; and the Engliſh Company had great cauſe to fear for their poſſeſſions. But they were fortunate in having ſome of the beſt officers in the univerſe; men whoſe intrepidity of ſoul was equal to any enterprize. Watſon and Clive had diſlodged the famous pirate Angria, from all his ſtrong holds on the Malabar, and were ſo luckily weak in men, that the Company could not hold them: they were, therefore, fortunately for us, given up to the Mahrattas, for a ſmall conſideration. Soon after the ſquadron had reached the Coromandel coaſt, the

troubles

troubles commenced in Bengal, from the causes above mentioned. Happily for the English, the Subah, a rash inexperienced young man, judged of the spirit of the whole English nation, from what he had seen of the irresolute behaviour of a few ill armed and undisciplined individuals at Fort William, and neglected to put an end to the war, by driving them entirely out of the country. He suffered them to collect together at a place called Fulta, about forty miles from Calcutta, and keep there in a body, until Watson and Clive could come to their relief. Then their knowledge of the country and language, and their just resentments, were of great use in the establishing of their affairs. But so far were they from thinking of making a conquest of Bengal, that I am confident, the English would very willingly have compounded with **the** Subah, for leave to resettle their factory on **the** former footing. Clive, who had studied the nature and genius of the Asiatics, and knew them better than any other European ever did, or perhaps ever will, soon discovered, that Surajah ul Dowlah was a Prince, on the faith of whose promises no dependence could be placed. This, and the news of a war having commenced between the French and English in Europe, determined the Admiral and the General, to dislodge the French from their settlement of Chandernagore, and carry the war into the heart of the Nabob's dominions, in order the sooner to bring him to reason.

THE

The following ten pages of the Abbé's fifth book, is such a rhapsody of extraordinary and contradictory assertions, that I have not penetration enough to comprehend what principle it is that he wishes to inculcate.—The interior parts of Hindoostan can, and cannot, be easily conquered. It may, and it may not, be easily held by Europeans.—The natives are, and are not, good soldiers.—Their armies are, and are not, formidable.—In short, it seems to me, that the Author of the History of the East and West Indies, possesses a most fertile and creative imagination, and that his principal study is to dress his ideas up in beautiful flowing language, totally regardless whether his assertions correspond with, or run counter to each other. I have not hitherto been able to discover from the Abbé's works, whether he hath personally visited any particular country, or studied the genius or character of any particular people in their own country. But I am confident he never was in Hindoostan: or if he was, he took on hearsay, all that he has written on that famous part of the world, and might as well have staid at home. When a writer uses the dogmatical stile on subjects of which he is master, truth compensates for the manner in which it is conveyed; but it is intolerable when made the vehicle of ignorance, or wilful misrepresentation. The Abbé's countryman, Bernier, in his writings, both instructs and pleases. He wrote of what he saw, and what he knew; and

has

has left behind him the best account of Hindoostan any where to be met with.

A NEUTRALITY between the European nations in India, whilst they are at war with each other in Europe, is too ridiculous an idea to merit consideration; nor can I conceive for what purpose the Abbé introduced it, any more than I can his other chimerical idea, of wishing the states of Europe might become one great mercantile commonwealth, except to shew the moderation and humanity of his disposition. But I am not ill pleased to find so learned a man, agreeing so entirely with me, that the military spirit is destructive of the mercantile; and that neglect of first principles, hath been the ruin of both the Portugueze and French trade in India; because I hope it will be a strong inducement to the English to avoid their mistakes, by pursuing a different conduct.

I AM totally indifferent whether the other European nations adopt the Abbé's medium plan of conducting their Asiatic trade, by companies without charters, or by individuals, as their subjects shall see fit, providing the English nation does not adopt it. He proves, beyond contradiction, that the distance which Europe is placed from India, and other difficulties which inevitably arise from the nature of the trade, that it is impossible for individuals to carry it on, without injury to the

country

country to which they belong, and ruin to themselves. That let what European nation soever, attempt the Indian trade by small companies, or individuals, they will naturally, and for their own security, unite at last. This the Abbé says, is the opinion and practice of all the trading nations in Europe, who have any communication by sea to Asia. Is it not surprising that the author, after having made this appear, by instancing such facts, that no one man can doubt of them, should propose to take away the only barrier, which the wisdom of ages hath hitherto been able to invent, to prevent the evils which the adventurous mercantile infatuation of individuals would cause to flow in upon us, the exclusive charter? Individuals, and small companies, of the same country, says the Abbé, will ruin one another. All nations by experience, have found it to be so. The remedy was to constitute a company, whose stock should be sufficient to carry on as much trade to Asia, as the interest of the particular nation to which the company belonged, could bear. To prevent individual rivals, who had hitherto distressed the company, injured their country, and ruined themselves, exclusive charters were granted. What security doth the Abbé offer, that the evils will not return, when the remedy is taken away? Is the spirit of adventure, formerly so conspicuous in individual European merchants, now no more? Until the Abbé proves that it is, I hope the English nation will have the wisdom

wisdom to conduct her Asiatic trade by the medium of one great, chartered, well regulated company.

SINCE the discovery of the passage by the Cape of Good Hope to Asia, no European nation hath ever possessed such mercantile advantages as the English nation now doth, from the situation of her settlements in India. The well combining and conducting of those advantages, is what, I think, they have hitherto been very inattentive to. The **trade from** India to India, as the Abbé calls it, is certainly **of** national utility, when indulged to free **merchants,** free mariners, and other individuals, who have found the way to India; but it often languishes in their hands in particular parts, to the great prejudice of the whole. The prosperity of of Bengal, is of the highest national importance to **Great** Britain. It flourishes or decays, as its ex**port** trade is well or ill managed. At present, the exports to the other parts of Asia, is solely in the hands of individuals, and they are not competent to the **good** management of it. Instead of restrictions, every indulgence should be given them; and some of the branches, the Company should themselves attend to. Of these branches I have said something in the First Letter. I have yet a great deal more to say on the same subject, when it comes **under** consideration.

The French, Danish, and Portugueze nations, trade to India much on the same terms that the English and Dutch now do to China; they import sufficient of the commodities of that distant country, to serve their own internal consumption. The French aim at more. They wish to share with the maritime powers, a part of the advantages arising from the re-exportation trade. Nor do I think it possible for the wit of man, to devise a plan more likely to effect that purpose, than that which the Abbé proposes. The Dutch supply all Europe with spices. It is now in the power of the English, to supply all Europe with the commodities of Bengal, excepting the nations above mentioned, who trade there for themselves; nor would I wish to see them deprived of that natural priviledge, to which they have a right, in times of peace, by the laws of God and man. But as one or other of the nations of Europe, who trade to India, must have the advantage of supplying with Asiatic commodities, Turkey, Russia, the Empire, and many other states who do not trade by sea to Asia, it is fair, just, and found mercantile policy in the English, to secure, from the lucky circumstances of their favourable situation, those advantages to themselves.

Before the conquest of Bengal by the English, all the nations of Europe, who traded to that kingdom, brought silver to make good the balance against them. They may, with proper management,

ment, be forced to bring it again; and bring it they should, or stay away.

There are established standards for the quality and goodness of all the articles of merchandize in every civilized part of the world. Those of Bengal are well known, both for the Europe and Asiatic markets; all of which, that can be wrought up to those standards, the natives should find a ready sale for, at the English Company's warehouses in Calcutta, and in the provinces; and they should send them to every market in Asia and Europe, where there could a vend be found for them. What ever you receive for those goods, is the neat proceeds of their industry. Would you wish a richer mine of real wealth? Not all those possessed by the Spaniards, from California to the Straits of Maghellan, on one side of the great American continent, or by the Spaniards and Portugueze, from the Gulf of Mexico to Cape Horn, on the other, is a millioneth part so valuable. In working their mines, they depopulate whole regions, and debase human nature below the brute creation. In working of yours, you multiply the human race, and give to millions a taste of liberty and independence. Make freedom flourish, where, until your arrival, the word was not understood. And in doing this, you, at the same time, raise your nation to a higher degree of opulence, than any other people hath hitherto experienced on the face of the earth. Two millions of Bengal goods, imported into the River of London, produces fifty times the national utility, that ten millions of silver, brought home by the Spanish galleons to Cadiz, doth to Spain.

NAVIGATION and trade is the proper motto to the arms of Britainnia; a bale of cloth, and a hogshead of sugar, her supporters; wool, raw-silk, pepper, calicoes, and tobacco, shine bright in the quarters; a code of her own jurisprudence, and a bag of wheat, make her a soft cushion; and a line of battle ship, the most glorious crest in the universe.

It is absolutely an act of madness, the keeping up such military establishments, as the English now do on the Malabar and Coromandel coast. They continually distress the Company; and the more you conquer, the more will that distress increase. To continue always armed, because you may at some future time possibly be attacked, is weakening yourselves, whilst your enemy grows stronger by being at peace.

BEFORE the war which commenced in 1756, Bombay, and the Company's other settlements on the Malabar coast, bore their own expences, and transmitted to Europe, a very considerable balance.

Some

Some years it amounted to an entire cargo of pepper. At present, they cost the Company immense sums annually. In short, there is no kind of economy; for as the Bombay servants have only to draw on Bengal for supplies, and the Company order they should be supplied, without caring what they do with the money, how can it be otherwise? Is there a Director in Leadenhall-Street, who knows that Mr. Hastings, since his accession to the government of Bengal, has supported their other settlements in India, with above a million sterling, and that mostly in cash? They never attended to this, nor to his representation, that such heavy drains, made constantly in ready money, or by bill, must in the end be destructive to Bengal. Do they know, that he has paid off a heavy debt of a million and a half more, which he found due on bond on his coming to their chair? Do they know, that from Bengal he has supplied them in Europe, with more than sufficient to pay off all their debts at home, although it amounted to near three millions, when he took their affairs in hand? And lastly, do they know, that there is at this moment, March the 25th, 1777, more than one million and a half sterling in their Bengal treasury? If they know all this, will they be so candid as to inform the public, on what principles the majority acted, when, in May 1776, after the ships of the season were dispatched, they voted an address to the King, to recall Mr. Hastings from his government?

ment? Hitherto we know not at Bengal, the upshot of that most iniquitous proceeding. I use that harsh appellation, because the measure deserved it. I call upon them in this public manner, to prove one single act of peculation, or mal-administration, on this great English Viceroy. Will they not hide their heads with shame and disgrace, when the whole nation shall know, that in the course of thirty months, which has elapsed since the selfish, brutal Clavering has been here, though he has had every villain in the country, both Europeans and natives, in his service, to suborn evidence, and invent stories, against the Governor General, that not one of the numerous charges, sent home by Clavering and his party, hath been proved against him in Asia or in Europe?

In the most solemn manner I declare, (and I sign my name to this paper, which the printer may shew to whom he pleases,) that I do believe, that in no period of time, did a stronger instance appear, which confirmed the maxim, that innocence alone, is sufficient support to a man in every situation of life, (if he does not desert himself,) than what has happened to Mr. Hastings in Bengal.

A word or two more with the Abbé Reynal, shall close this Letter. Who is it that does not see the secret drift of that laborious and, as it relates to Great Britain, inflammatory production? According

cording to the Abbe's account, England is a haughty and unjust rival to France, a false friend to Holland, a secret enemy to Spain, and a tyrant over Portugal. " Are the Portugueze to be com-
" pared to these upstarts, whose heads are turned
" by the embarrassment which their newly acquired
" riches occasion?" The last lines are in the Abbé's own words, as Justamond has translated them. They are to be found in book the ninth, page 527, of the second volume. I hate quotation of all kinds, and therefore must refer the reader to the whole work; in the perusal of which, if he doth not discover, that the principal view of the writer, is to inflame the great trading states in Europe against the English nation, I am extremely mistaken. If the States General could be brought to join the family compact, it is not unlikely, but a confederate war might be entered into by the four above mentioned powers against Great Britain. Such a combination would certainly not be a desirable one; but I see not that it is to be feared. It would have one good effect; it would unite us among ourselves, and then we should have little to dread from such a war. Passion and prejudice would not be sufficient to permit such a confederacy to draw together long, whose real interests are so different. If the Dutch and Portugueze are so infatuated, as not to discover at first, the secret designs of France, the capricious impatience of that volatile nation, will soon open their eyes. The Abbé has taken

great

great care to shew his countrymen, that the other four states have shared them almost entirely out in the eastern and western world; and that the most likely way for them to force themselves in for a better portion of the mercantile plumb-cake, is to inflame the minds of the Dutch, Spaniards, and Portugueze, against what he calls the rapacious greediness of the English, and thereby to set them all together by the years, that they may run away with great part of the spoil. The Abbé says there are circumstances and events, which, when well attended to, plainly foretel the great revolutions in states and governments; and he insinuates clearly enough, that he foresees the decline of the British empire. He gives the English some good advice, but then would wish it to be understood to mean, that it is now too late for them to follow it. I remember a countryman of the Abbé's, who, after the capture of Mahon, by the Duke de Richlieu, in the last war, applied the *delenda est Carthago* to Great Britain, as dogmatically and unprophetically, as the Abbé himself could do. His countrymen can intrigue, dress a wig, walk a minuet, and fight for half an hour, as well as any men upon earth; but then they have no bottom. Set their blood a running, and they run also. Old John ever hath, and ever will drub them. If Strut and Frog, and Tom the Dustman, interpose, to save Baboon from the cudgelling his restless petulance may give him a just title to expect, they will have to thank themselves

selves for their folly, if, in the fray, they get a broken pate, as Strut lately did, over which, to this hour, he wears a black patch. It may heal, if it is left to nature and to time. But if such state empirics as the Abbé, will be tampering, teizing, and fretting the part, and Bull, in his justly roused rage, should give them another butt, and knock the Havannah against Carthagena, or Mexico against Peru, or sink the whole in the great gulf of the British empire, of which the Abbé tells such dismal stories, who in the name of goodness will be able to prevent it? Not Louis, take my word for it. He will, in the day of trial, keep aloof from danger, as his well known and detested ancestor did, in the former naval wars, which he fomented between the maritime states, when the British diadem was sullied by the filthy brows of a libertine Stuart.

If the Abbé's History of the Indies, was to be translated into all the languages and dialects, which are spoken, and have been spoken, by the different people of whom he writes, from the days of the great Columbus to the present times, and some knowing and judicious men of each nation and community, were to strip him of all the false facts, and consequently false reasoning, established on them, which related to their own particular state or community, to what a snug little pocket companion would his voluminous works be reduced. I know he is wrong in a great number of the facts, he so dogmatically relates of the affairs transacted in the East Indies, and that lessens my confidence in him, when I read his account of other people, and other nations, of whom I know nothing. Yet so indolent and indifferent are mankind in general, as to matters which do not relate immediately to themselves, or their friends, that they swallow with great avidity, every story that is conveyed to them in such harmonious and correct language, in which, I am told, the original is written. If Mr. Hastings lives, I hope an honest history of Hindoostan from his pen. If not, surely there are in the nation, men of honour and abilities, who have public spirit enough to search the national and Company's records, and apply to numbers of men yet alive, and from them collect materials sufficient to refute the hasty and undigested assertions of this French Abbé. Were I as equal to the task as many men I know, who have served their country in India, I should think it indispensably my duty, as an Englishman, to undertake it. Impotent as I am, and weak in learning and natural abilities, I will, from time to time, bring to the test some of the Abbé's mistakes, in the course of these Letters, and that is all I can do.

www.ingramcontent.com/pod-product-compliance
Lightning Source LLC
Chambersburg PA
CBHW031824230426
43669CB00009B/1218